BREAD BAKING BASICS

BREAD BAKING BASICS

Recipes for Mastering Bread, Dough and Flour

Recipes, Photos and Illustrations

BY GREGORY BERGER

Turner Publishing Company
Nashville, Tennessee
www.turnerpublishing.com

Copyright © 2021 Gregory Berger

Baking Bread Basics: Recipes for Mastering Bread, Dough and Flour

No part of this publication may be reproduced, stored in a retrieval system, or transmitted in any form or by any means, electronic, mechanical, photocopying, recording, scanning, or otherwise, except as permitted under Sections 107 or 108 of the 1976 United States Copyright Act, without either the prior written permission of the Publisher, or authorization through payment of the appropriate per-copy fee to the Copyright Clearance Center, 222 Rosewood Drive, Danvers, MA 01923, (978) 750-8400, fax (978) 750-4744. Requests to the Publisher for permission should be addressed to Turner Publishing Company, 4507 Charlotte Avenue, Suite 100, Nashville, Tennessee, 37209, (615) 255-2665, fax (615) 255-5081, E-mail: admin@turnerpublishing.com.

Limit of Liability/Disclaimer of Warranty: While the publisher and the author have used their best efforts in preparing this book, they make no representations or warranties with respect to the accuracy or completeness of the contents of this book and specifically disclaim any implied warranties of merchantability or fitness for a particular purpose. No warranty may be created or extended by sales representatives or written sales materials. The advice and strategies contained herein may not be suitable for your situation. You should consult with a professional where appropriate. Neither the publisher nor the author shall be liable for any loss of profit or any other commercial damages, including but not limited to special, incidental, consequential, or other damages.

Cover photography: © Gregory Berger
Photos and Illustrations: © Gregory Berger
Cover, Layout & Design: Morgane Leoni

Library of Congress Cataloging-in-Publication number: 2021935937
ISBN: (print) 978-1-64250-570-2, (ebook) 978-1-64250-571-9
BISAC Category Code CKB009000, COOKING / Courses & Dishes / Bread

Printed in the United States of America

CONTENTS

PART 1 / BARE CUPBOARD BAKING — 8
    Start Today — 10

PART 2 / LET'S GO — 12
    Bread Basics — 13
    Notes on Equipment — 14
    Notes on Ingredients — 17
    Notes on Terms and Techniques — 18
    A Quick Breakdown of Baking a Loaf of Bread — 19

PART 3 / FRESH BREADS, DAILY — 24
    Just a Loaf of White Bread — 26
    Whole Lotta Wheat Bread — 29
    The Easiest Burger Bun — 30
    Furikake Pita Breads — 33
    Big, Fat Biscuits — 34
    Soft Pretzels & Pretzel Bites — 37
    Blueberry Almond Muffins with Crumbly Top — 38
    Chocolate Cherry Almond Scones — 41
    Japanese Milk Bread — 42
    Hokkaido Milk Rolls — 45
    Señorita Bread — 46
    Tin Can Bread — 49
    Quick and Easy Flatbreads — 50

PART 4 / RISE UP! — 52
    No-Knead Artisan Cheddar Jalapeño Bread — 54
    Green Onion Pullman Bread — 57
    Perfect Pizza Crust — 61
    Challah — 62
    Blueberry Donuts — 65
    Blueberry Cream Cheese Babka — 66
    Croissants Two Ways — 69
        Pain au Chocolat — 74
        Ham and Swiss Croissants with Thyme — 75
    Buttermilk Cinnamon Rolls with Cinnamon Icing — 77
    Conchas — 78
    Lemon, Rosemary, Tomato Focaccia — 81
    Candied Orange Pretzeled Bagels — 82
        Candied Orange Peels — 83

PART 5 / GLUTEN, OUT! — 86
    Gluten-Free Baking — 88
    Gluten-Free Focaccia — 90
    Gluten-Free Pizza Dough — 93
    Gluten-Free Artisan Loaf — 94

PART 6 / THIS IS COMMITMENT — 96
    Wait! Are You a Scientist? — 99
    Sourdough Starter — 101
    Award-Winning Sourdough — 105
        Cinnamon Raisin Sourdough — 110
        Lemon, Rosemary, and Pine Nut Sourdough — 111
        Coconut, Cherry, and Walnut Sourdough — 112
        Cheddar and Jalapeño Sourdough — 113

Sourdough English Muffins	114
Sourdough Crackers	117

PART 7 / BREAD IDEAS — 118

Bread Ideas	120
Breadcrumbs	122
Croutons	123
Fried Green Tomatoes with Pickled Corn & Peppers	124
Sweet Pickle Rémoulade	124
Quick Pickled Corn & Chili Pepper Relish	125
Watermelon, Tomato Panzanella	127
Heirloom Tomato Vinaigrette	127
Grilled Soft Pretzel with Turkey and Cheese	129
Open-Face Tomato Sandwich	130
Avocado Toast	132
Focaccia BLT	133
Corn, Chiles and Tomato Toasts	134
Lemon Ricotta Spread	137
Japanese Eggplant Spread	138
The Summer Classic Burger	141
Corn & Chile Peppers	141
Tiny Potato Party	142
Savory Bread Pudding	145
Berry Bread Pudding	146
Concha Bread Pudding	149
Pizza, Pizza!	150
Salami, Pineapple, and Corn Pizza	151
Pear, Brie, and Onions	152
BBQ, Pickled Corn and Peppers, Sausage	152
Potato, Bacon and Blue	153
Fig, Goat Cheese, and Bacon	154
Pretzel Tray Dippers	155
Honey Mustard	155
Jalapeño IPA Cheese	155
Ranch!	155
Señorita Bread Waffles	159
Strawberry Shortcakes	160

ACKNOWLEDGEMENTS	162
ABOUT THE AUTHOR	163
MY FAVORITE BREAD RESOURCES	164
INDEX	165

PART 1
BARE CUPBOARD BAKING

I wanted to write a bread baking book that takes away all the things that makes baking hard for people who just want some tasty bread. No digital scales to measure the flours in grams or ounces. No thermometers to measure the temperature of your resting dough. No flours that you can only find in specialty stores. There are plenty of books that will take you deeper in that world of baking. Here, it's flour, water, yeast, salt, eggs, butter, milk. Staples that we can turn into bread for our family.

There are few smells that bring up the feeling of warmth and comfort like fresh-baked bread. Toast with a little butter can be as warm as a hug from grandma. The sight of a coiled cinnamon roll can bring you back to the State Fair when you were a kid. A fresh-baked burger bun can welcome in the sunshine of summer on a cold winter's day.

The world had a reawakening in 2020 with our food system. During the initial lockdowns, flour and yeast quickly disappeared from store shelves. America panic-bought all the toilet paper and active dry yeast, which, looking back, was a super strange combination. A few weeks in, I started to get texts from people asking if I had yeast or sourdough starter to give them. I'm almost always stocked up in the baking supplies department, so I gladly dropped off baggies of yeast on porches, as well as small tubs of sourdough starter.

When the yeast ran out, I turned back to sourdough along with a lot of other folks. You can make sourdough starter with just flour and water, without the store-bought yeast, but it's a process. I started getting so many requests about how to do it that I began filming Instagram stories walking people through the whole process. Sometimes, I'd have up to a one hundred people watching along, trying it at home. I would get instant messages with starter photos asking, "Is this right?! What do I do next?"

There is a joy to being able to take a few standard ingredients and bake them into something so beautiful as a loaf of bread, a loaf that can provide nourishment, comfort, and well-being to whoever it's for.

I want to teach you how to bake the best breads with the simplest ingredients, probably with what you already have in your cupboard.

I WANT YOU TO HAVE FRESH BREAD, DAILY. SO, LET'S GO BAKE.

START TODAY

Our house is filled with self-improvement books, little books filled with inspirational messages, day-to-day calendars with tiny messages of hope. Most say things like, "a friend in need is a friend indeed," which is true, or a quote about checking up on Eeyore, which we probably should also go do. But one morning, I flipped open a book and the page just said, "TODAY COUNTS."

Say it out loud, "TODAY COUNTS!" It is one of your days. You only have so many, and this is one of them. We all have special days that we look forward to—birthdays, holidays, even weekends. But today holds the same opportunities as the one you are looking forward to. It counts as one of your days. There are no warm-up days, no do-over days, we've already done those. These are the days.

Have you been putting something off that you'll do when you have a little more time? Learning to knit? Play the ukulele? Learn to bake sourdough? I'm here to tell you, start today. Life is a process, and we need to learn and practice and take chances. I've heard so many people say they love baking and want to learn, but just haven't done it yet. There is an initial investment for equipment, but after that, if you can find flour and time, you'll be churning out golden loaves in no time.

When you break your day down into small chunks, you just may find that there really is time to do something else. Look for the things that are stealing your time (hint: it's your phone). Baking is a time commitment, but if you read the recipes ahead of time and plan out the timing, the actual hand-on time needed is pretty minimal. You'll be cranking out golden loaves in no time!

So this is your lucky day. Come on! I'll show you how, and I'll try to leave out the intimidating stuff and we'll just make some really good bread. It may not work the first time. It may not work perfectly the fifth time. But it will work if you keep moving forward.

PART 2
LET'S GO

There is a lot of science behind bread baking, and if you want to become a professional baker and make loaves for a living, you need to learn all the terms and understand on a microbial level all that is happening when you add the warm liquid to the yeast. But if you just want to make a loaf of bread for your kid? Make some darn good cinnamon rolls? You just need to know some basic things.

Timing is the most important thing. Time management! To be successful in baking, you need to read the full recipe and plan your day or days accordingly. Some of the recipes here take, start to finish, a few hours, and some, like the sourdough and croissants, take DAYS to make. It's never a lot of work each day, it's a little here and little there with lots of space between.

In the bread world, there are lots of terms like hydration, autolyse, baker's percentages, benching, biga, bulk fermentation, poolish, leaven… I've tried to leave all those out of this book and just show you how to bake bread. There are a few main things you need to know to get started.

BREAD BASICS

HAPPY YEAST

Make sure your yeast is still good. If you are using the yeast packets you found in the cupboard, there's a good chance they have gone bad. Yeast packets are generally good for about two years, so if you don't remember buying it? Probably time to buy some new yeast, preferably in a jar so you can measure it out better. Give it a test run if you've had it for a long time. Sprinkle a small amount of yeast into some warm water. If it starts to foam up and smell yeasty, it's good. When in doubt, throw it out.

MIX IT UP

When you are mixing doughs, make sure everything gets mixed and there are no pockets of dry flour. Most of these doughs get mixed by the dough hook on a mixer or stretched and folded by hand.

REST

We all need rest, right? It's important that if the recipe says, "rest for thirty minutes," you let that happen. Some of the recipes call for overnight rests. During those long rests, we are actually fermenting the bread, which is allowing the yeast time to eat the sugars in the flour and turn them into small amounts of alcohol and carbon dioxide. This is also making them taste really good! For recipes like pizza dough, the longer you keep in the refrigerator, the better, up to a few days.

STAY IN SHAPE

The folding and shaping of the dough is also very important. Most of the time, the folding is done to help trap gasses while it's baking to then give the bread lift. The surfaces of the breads need to have a surface tension to help rise. For items with a more complex shaping or folding technique, I've included illustrations or photos to show how it's done.

HOW HOT?

Oven temperatures are tricky. You probably should, every once in a while, test the temperature of your oven to see if it runs hot or cold. Heat it to 350°F with an oven thermometer in it and see if the two temperatures match up. Even with a properly calibrated oven, keep an eye on your breads as they bake. You may need to rotate the pans halfway through if parts of the breads are baking faster than others.

NOTES ON EQUIPMENT

Most of the recipes here require a few basic pieces of equipment.

CUTTING BOARD

You are going to need a big cutting board or clean, flat surface. I have a large, wooden cutting board that I only use for rolling out dough. I've found that when you use a board that you've cut onions or garlic on, even if you've scrubbed the heck out of it, sometimes those flavors penetrate the dough. I just avoid that altogether by having a dedicated bread board.

LOAF PANS

For the bread recipes that use a loaf pan to bake in, I've used the same nine-by-four-inch aluminum baking pan for all of them. I have two of them, so I can double up on bread by baking both of them at the same time. The Green Onion Pullman Bread on page 57 uses a special Pullman loaf pan. It's essentially just a loaf pan but has a sliding lid on it. You can find these online or at restaurant supply store. If you have pans that are slightly smaller or slightly larger than four by nine inches, they should still work just fine.

BENCH SCRAPER

A bench scraper will help you get sticky dough off the cutting boards. I have a cheap plastic one that works great. You can get nicer metal ones with wooden handles, but it's not necessary. I think the plastic versions work a little better, especially for beginners, because they have a little give to them. You can get away without one, but they are pretty cheap and will help in the long run.

BIG OLD BOWL

A big bowl is necessary for a snug place for your dough to rise. I have a nice ceramic bowl my friend Sandy made that I always use for rising dough. It's just one of those things...

if you are happy and inspired by the bowl, maybe your dough will be happier, too.

STANDING MIXER

The biggest equipment expense is that most of the recipes use a standing mixer with a dough hook. I use a KitchenAid that I've had for years. Obviously, people have made bread for centuries without a standing mixer, and you can, too. You can just stir and knead and stir and knead. But if you plan on making bread a lot, a standing mixer will become a very good friend in your kitchen.

BAKING SHEETS

For baking sheets, I use sixteen-by-twenty-inch rimmed sheets. I have a few so I can have dough rising and baking at the same time. I use four sheets that are all the same size. That way, for some recipes like the croissants, I can have two sheets baking in the oven while two other sheets are being used to proof the remaining croissants.

PARCHMENT

Precut parchment paper is one of my favorite kitchen inventions. I buy a big pack of two hundred sheets at a time. I get sixteen-by-twenty-inch sheets that fit perfectly onto my rimmed baking sheets. The ease of having these precut parchment sheets saves a lot of time and you won't need to grease your baking sheets. Silicone sheets work well too but are more expensive.

BLADES

To make the slashes across the tops of bread, I just use a razor blade. I buy a small box from the hardware store and make sure they become "kitchen only" tools. You can buy what's called a "lame" which is really a sharp blade on a stick, but, to me, buying extra things is kind of unnecessary. A sharp razor blade works great.

COOLING RACKS

Cooling racks are a good idea so you can remove the loaves and baked goods from the hot pans and baking sheets and have them cool without drying out.

BANNETON PROOFING BASKETS

Bannetons are round or oval shaped bamboo baskets that help your loaves hold their shape as they proof. In this book, we are only using them in the sourdough section. You can easily find them online, and you'll need two in order to make the two sourdough loaves at once. They have ridges that will also give your breads a nice artisan look. If you don't want to buy these, you can always line a bowl with a clean, non-fuzzy dish towel and use that instead, but you won't get the cool little lines in the sides of your loaves.

Other than that, with just a few measuring cups and spoons, you can begin your journey.

NOTES ON INGREDIENTS

YEAST

For all the yeasted bread recipes in this book, except for the sourdough section, I use active dry yeast. I found it's easier for beginning bakers to have a standard to get used to. Active dry yeast is easy to use and easy to find. Costco often sells a two-pound bag, which lasts me almost a full year, and I bake A LOT. I buy the two-pound bag, then transfer it to a large Mason jar and store it in the refrigerator. Keeping it in the jar and refrigerated keeps it fresh and happy and lasts a long time. You can buy the little packets, too, but buying a jar or the two-pound bag gives you more control of how much you are using and is more cost effective.

My recommendation for the highest chance of success with this book it to buy some new yeast before you start. Yeast is a living thing, and if you are pulling out a strip of packets that have been in your cupboard for ten years, they probably aren't going to work. So start new. You can test the health of your yeast by sprinkling a small amount of yeast into some warm water. If it starts to foam up and smell yeasty, it's good.

FLOUR

There are so many flour types out there, but because this is a book for baking beginners, I've stuck with regular old all-purpose flour and whole wheat flour. Because I bake a lot, I order fifty-pound bags directly from the mill, so I always have some on hand.

Once you get the hang of baking, experiment with different flours. Find a local miller if you can and try out heirloom grains. They can be expensive, so I like to master the recipe with all-purpose flour before I try an heirloom grain. The heirlooms are especially good in sourdough.

GLUTEN-FREE FLOUR

In the gluten-free section, I have some notes on the flours I used. Again, I think it's best to buy the least expensive all-purpose gluten-free flour to get the hang of it. Then once you have a feel for gluten-free baking, try buying each component of gluten-free flour, and make your own custom blend. It's generally a mix of white and brown rice flours, then a blend of tapioca, millet, potato starch, and a binder like xanthan gum.

SALT

All the recipes here use fine grain sea salt when adding salt into the dough. Some recipes call for flake salt to go on top, and for that I use Maldon or Jacobsen sea salt flakes. The soft pretzels need pretzel salt, which can be found online.

WATER AND MILK

All the water used is tap water. All the milk I used is 2 percent, but any milk will do. Just note, using a nut milk will not produce the same results as cow's milk. When I say warm water or warm milk, it means you can dip your finger in it and not yank it out. You want it warm enough to activate the yeast, but if it's too hot, you'll kill your little yeast buddies.

BUTTER AND EGGS

All the butter I used is unsalted butter. But get this, if you only have salted, just go for it. It won't make a huge difference. For the eggs, they are all cage-free large eggs. A lot of recipes I've read say to bring your eggs to room temperature, but seriously, who thinks that far ahead? I've never brought an egg to room temperature before using.

NOTES ON TERMS AND TECHNIQUES

PROOFING & FERMENTATION

Proofing is the part in the bread making process where you are letting the shaped dough sit undisturbed, and the yeast keep working away, making it rise a little more. The first rise is really called bulk fermentation, but it's really just leaving the dough alone and rising. When I say proof time, I'm combining these two terms. If the recipe says, "Proof Time: 2 hours" it combines the bulk fermentation and the final proofing into one number, so you can easily see how long it needs to sit quietly.

ACTIVATING YEAST

Some of the recipes here have you add the yeast right into the flour and other ingredients, and the yeast gets activated by the warm ingredients. Other times, we give the yeast a boost by doing an initial activation that involves mixing the warm liquid used in the recipe with the sugar and the yeast and letting it sit for a few minutes.

MIXING AND KNEADING

Most of the recipes use a standing mixer to mix to knead the dough. If you don't have one, kneading the dough is the way to go. To knead, place your dough on a floured surface. Press away from yourself with the heels of your hands, then turn the dough ninety degrees, fold it in half, then press again away from you with the heels of your hands. Repeat. Keep this up until you have a nice, smooth dough, roughly for as long as the recipe calls for mixing with the dough hook. This is a great arm workout.

A QUICK BREAKDOWN OF BAKING A LOAF OF BREAD

THIS IS THE SIMPLE STEP-BY-STEP BREAKDOWN OF MAKING JUST A LOAF OF WHITE BREAD
Full recipe on page 26

1. GET YOUR INGREDIENTS IN ORDER

It may not be necessary to say this, but read the recipe and make sure you have everything you need before you begin.

2. ACTIVATE THE YEASTIES

Mix the yeast in a bowl with the warm liquid (usually water or milk) and a sweetener (usually honey or sugar). Let sit for a few minutes until it's foamy.

3. MIX IT UP

Add the liquid yeast to the dry ingredients and mix. Leave the mixer going, or knead by hand, until the dough is smooth and elastic.

4. RISE UP!

This the called bulk fermentation, but it's really just leaving the dough alone and letting it rise. It'll double in size.

5. SHAPE IT

Now, we scrape the dough out onto a board and gently shape the loaf. Flatten it out, roll it up, then place in the greased pan.

6. PROOF

Let the dough sit again, now in its final shape, to rise back up again.

7. BAKE

The pan goes into the oven to bake. Once it's baked and golden brown, be sure to let it cool before slicing!

PART 3
FRESH BREADS, DAILY

RECIPES FROM START TO FINISH IN ABOUT FOUR HOURS

JUST A LOAF OF WHITE BREAD

Prep time: **20 minutes**
Proof time: **1.5 hours**
Bake time: **30–35 minutes**
Makes **1 big loaf**

2 cups water, warmed
1½ teaspoons active dry yeast
2 tablespoons sugar
1 teaspoon salt
3 tablespoons unsalted butter, softened
5 cups all-purpose flour

Sometimes you just want a regular ole slice of white bread. This is super easy and really quick to make. It's a perfect loaf for PB&J, grilled cheese, or cinnamon toast.

- In a small bowl, heat the water until warm to the touch, and stir in the yeast. Let sit for about 5 minutes until foamy.
- In mixer bowl, add in the sugar, salt, and flour. With the mixer on slow and using the dough hook, mix the dry ingredients and slowly pour in the warm water and yeast mixture. Add in two tablespoons of butter (reserving the last tablespoon for later). Mix until the dough becomes a soft ball and stops sticking to the sides of the bowl, about 5 minutes. When ready, cover the bowl with a towel and let the dough rise for an hour until doubled in size.
- Grease the inside of a nine-by-four-inch loaf pan with butter or oil. Gently turn the dough out onto a floured surface and flatten out into a large rectangle about a half-inch thick. Starting at the shorter end, tightly roll the dough into a tube. Pinch the ends down and fold under. Carefully lift the dough and place seam sides down in the pan. Tuck any weird areas down. Cover with a towel and let rise again for about a half hour.
- Preheat oven to 400°F. Brush the top of the loaf with the remaining melted butter, place in oven, and bake for about 30–35 minutes until golden brown. Remove from oven and brush with a little more butter. Let cool before slicing!

WHOLE LOTTA WHEAT BREAD

Prep time: **20 minutes**
Proof time: **2 hours**
Bake time: **30 minutes**
Makes **1 loaf**

1½ cups water, warmed
2 teaspoons active dry yeast
1 tablespoon honey
2 teaspoons salt
1 tablespoon olive oil
1 cup all-purpose flour
3½ cups whole wheat flour
Milk for brushing before baking

This makes a denser loaf of bread than the white bread loaves but is loaded with healthier whole wheat flour. A touch of honey sweetens it up. Try sprinkling oats over the top for an even better presentation. My kid doesn't like the oats on top, so we leave it blank.

- In a small bowl, heat the water until warm to the touch and stir in the yeast and honey. Let sit for about 5 minutes until foamy.
- In a large bowl, add in 1 cup of all-purpose flour and 1 cup of the whole wheat. Pour in the water yeast mixture, stir to make a thick batter, then lit sit, covered, for about 45 minutes.
- Add in the salt and oil, then slowing stir in the other 2½ cups of whole wheat flour. When the flour is incorporated, mix in the stand mixer with a dough hook on medium speed for about 8 minutes until it forms a smooth dough.
- Place in an oiled bowl, cover with a towel, and let the dough rise for 45 more minutes until doubled in size. Punch it down, and let it rise again for another 45 minutes.
- Grease the inside of a nine-by-four-inch loaf pan with butter or oil. Gently turn the dough out onto a floured surface and flatten out into a large rectangle about a half-inch thick. Starting at the shorter end, tightly roll the dough into a tube. Pinch the ends down and fold under. Carefully lift the dough and place seam sides down in the pan. Tuck any weird areas down. Cover with a towel and let rise again for about a half hour.
- Preheat oven to 350°F. Brush the top of the loaf with milk, slash the top with a sharp knife, then place in oven and bake for about 55 minutes until golden brown. Remove from oven and brush with a little butter. Let cool before slicing!

Prep time: **20 minutes**
Proof time: **about 2½ hours**
Bake time: **15–18 minutes**
Makes **8 buns**

THE EASIEST BURGER BUN

1 cup water, warmed
2 teaspoons active dry yeast
2 tablespoons unsalted butter, cold, cut into pieces
1 large egg
3½ cups all-purpose flour
¼ cup sugar
1¼ teaspoons salt
1 egg yolk (for egg wash)

There's nothing like Burger Night with fresh-baked buns. Got a few hours before dinner? Get these going by two o'clock and you can have fresh buns by dinnertime!

- In the mixer bowl, stir together everything except the egg yolk for the wash. Mix with the dough hook for about 5 minutes or until the mix is a smooth ball.
- Sometimes, the ball will be a few smaller balls. Pack them into one ball with your hands, then cover with a towel for about 1 hour or until it's doubled in size.
- Divide the dough into 8 pieces. Do your best to roll each piece into a smooth ball. It helps to kind of fold the dough over itself to make the top side of the bun a tight, smooth surface. Make sure you place it seam side down on the parchment.
- Place buns onto two parchment-lined baking sheets, 4 per sheet. Lightly cover and let rise for about 1½ hours or until very puffy.
- Preheat oven to 375°F.
- Lightly brush each bun with egg yolk (mix a yolk with a few drops of water). Add any seeds at this point or go without.
- Place in oven and bake for about 15–18 minutes or until golden brown. Let cool on wire racks.

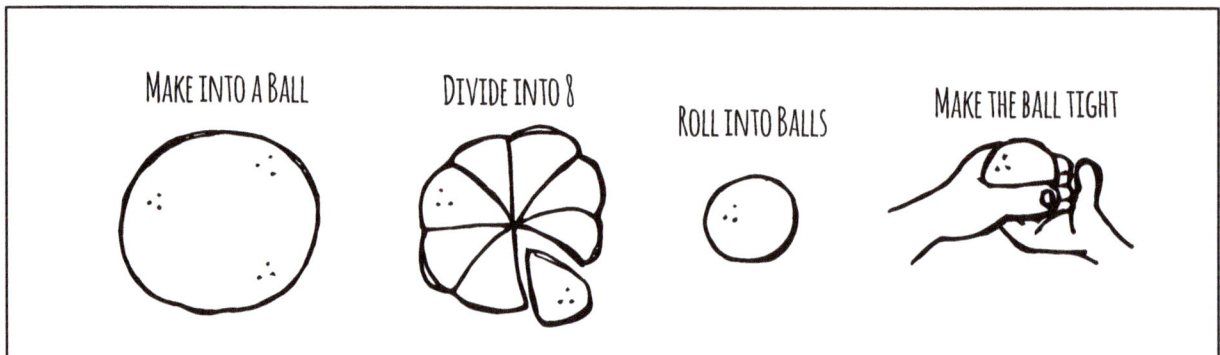

Make into a Ball Divide into 8 Roll into Balls Make the Ball Tight

FURIKAKE PITA BREADS

Prep time: **15 minutes**
Proof time: **about 2 hours**
Bake time: **3–5 minutes each**
Makes **8 pitas**

1 cup water, warmed
2 teaspoons active dry yeast
3 cups all-purpose flour
2 tablespoons furikake seasoning
2 teaspoons salt

A little bit of the Japanese seasoning blend called furikake takes these pitas to a whole new level with bits of dried seaweed and sesame seeds. You can find furikake seasoning at most grocery stores. I used Trader Joe's Nori Komi Furikake blend. Pitas are a pretty easy bread to master, but it does require some patience. Any extra pitas can be turned into pita pizzas or chopped up and toasted to make salad croutons. You can just leave out the furikake seasoning to make a plain pita.

- In the mixer bowl, stir together all the ingredients. Mix with the dough hook to combine, then mix on low for about 5-7 minutes.
- Lightly oil a separate bowl and scoop out dough into this new bowl. Move the dough ball so it's oiled all around, then cover with a towel for about 1-2 hours or until it's doubled in size.
- Put your baking stone, if you have one, into the oven first. If not, put a cookie sheet in. Preheat oven to 450°F.
- Divide the dough into 8 pieces and roll into balls. On a floured surface with a rolling pin, flatten out the balls until they are about 8 inches across. If they shrink up on you, let them rest for a few minutes, then roll some more. They will eventually behave.
- Until you get the hang of it, toss one dough disk into the hot stone or cookie sheet one at a time. It should start to puff up like a whoopee cushion after about a minute. Flip it with tongs, then bake for about another minute. When it's fully puffed and starting to brown, slide it out with tongs and continue to cook the rest.
- Remember, a watched pita never puffs.

Prep time: **20 minutes**
Bake time: **20 minutes**
Makes **16 biscuits**

BIG, FAT BISCUITS

4½ cups all-purpose flour, plus more for dusting the surface
1 tablespoon baking powder
1 teaspoon baking soda
2 teaspoons sugar
1 teaspoon salt
1 cup unsalted butter, COLD
1½ to 2 cups buttermilk

This recipe uses a croissant technique to build up tons of flaky layers. Keep your butter cold and friends nearby. Serve these flaky beasts with homemade jam, honey, or just more butter.

- Preheat oven to 425°F. Line a baking sheet with parchment paper and set aside.
- In a large bowl, whisk together all the dry ingredients. Cut the cold butter into little squares and, using a fork or fingers, work the butter into the flour mix until it's coarse like crumbs. Fold in about 1½ cups of the buttermilk until you have a wet, sticky dough. If it's still kind of dry, add more buttermilk until it's all wet.
- Stick the bowl in the freezer now for about 10 minutes to cool it all back down. Keeping the butter cold is very important here, and your hot little hands probably warmed it up.
- Generously dust a cutting board with flour, and then dump out the wet mixture. With a rolling pin, roll out the dough into a rough rectangle shape. Fold ⅓ of the rectangle in on itself, then fold the other side over the folded part (like folding a letter). Roll this down flat, then do the letter fold again. Roll down, then fold. Do this roll and fold a total of six times (it'll be an arm workout toward the end!). Continue to dust your hands and the cutting board as you go, or you'll become a big, sticky mess.
- When done, gently roll the dough out again to about one-inch thickness.
- With a round cutter, cut biscuits into 2½-inch circles. Place on the baking sheet about an inch apart.
- Bake for 20 minutes. When done, brush the tops with melted butter.

Roll out flat | Fold 1/3 over | Fold other side over | Roll back out, cut circles out | See the layers?

Prep time: **30 minutes**
Proof time: **1 hour**
Bake time: **15 minutes**
(plus a few minutes to boil)
Makes **about 8 pretzels**

SOFT PRETZELS & PRETZEL BITES

NOTE

Makes about 8 pretzels, but it's all about how big or small you make them. You can also make little pretzel bites.

INGREDIENTS

1½ cups water, warmed
1 tablespoon sugar
2 teaspoons salt
2¼ teaspoons active dry yeast
4 cups all-purpose flour
2 tablespoons unsalted butter, melted

PRETZEL BOIL

8 cups water
½ cup baking soda

EGG WASH

1 egg yolk (mixed with 1 tablespoon water)
Pretzel salt

These are pretty easy to make and can be done in a short amount of time because they only have one rise and quick baking time. Serve them with Honey Mustard or a Jalapeño IPA Cheese Sauce (recipe on page 155).

- Mix the warm water in a bowl with the sugar and yeast. Let sit for a few minutes until foamy. In a mixing bowl with the dough hook, add the flour, salt, and melted butter. With mixer on, add the warm water and mix for about 5–7 minutes until dough has formed a smooth ball that's no longer sticking to the sides. Cover with a towel and let rise for about an hour until doubled in size.
- Preheat oven to 450°F. On stove top in a large pot, bring the 8 cups of water to a boil and add in the baking soda.
- On a cutting board, turn out your dough and divide into eight equal parts. One at a time, make snakes. Lay the snake out in a U shape, then take the ends and fold over each other to form a pretzel shape. Do this to all eight. If you want to make pretzels bites instead, chop the snakes into 1-inch-long pieces at this point.
- Two at a time, drop the pretzels into the boiling water and boil for about 30 seconds. With a slotted spoon, remove them and place on a parchment-lined baking sheet. Repeat with all the rest of the pretzels or pretzel bites. Brush the boiled pretzels with the egg yolk mixture and top with pretzel salt.

NOTE: Regular salt won't work here. If you don't have access to pretzel salt, try topping with shredded cheese and oregano for a pizza pretzel.

- Bake in oven for about 15 minutes until dark golden brown. These are best eaten right away.

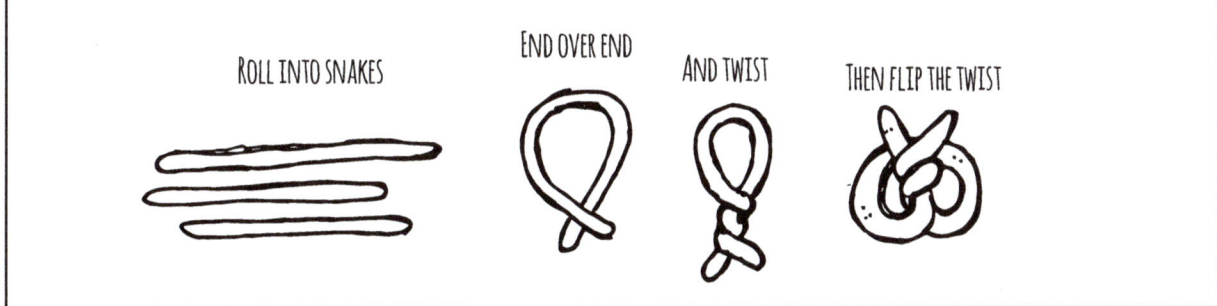
Roll into snakes — End over end — And twist — Then flip the twist

BLUEBERRY ALMOND MUFFINS WITH CRUMBLY TOP

Prep time: **10 minutes**
Bake time: **22 minutes**
Makes **12 muffins**

MUFFIN INGREDIENTS

¾ cup unsweetened applesauce
⅔ cup sugar
2 large eggs
⅓ cup coconut oil, softened
2 teaspoons almond extract
1½ cups all-purpose flour
¼ teaspoon baking powder
½ teaspoon baking soda
1 tablespoon cinnamon
½ teaspoon salt
½ cup oats
½ cup fresh or frozen blueberries

CINNAMON TOPPER

⅛ cup flour
¼ cup sugar
1 teaspoon cinnamon
1 tablespoon butter, melted

These little muffins are adaptable to just about any season. If blueberries are too expensive or you just want to try something different, substitute with strawberries, cherries, apples, or bananas (did someone say chocolate chips?).

TO MAKE TOPPER

- Make sure butter is melted, then mix all the ingredients together.

FOR THE MUFFINS

- Preheat oven to 350°F.
- In a large bowl, add all the ingredients and mix until just smooth.
- Oil a muffin tin with nonstick spray, or prepare a muffin tin with paper liners.
- Divide the mix equally into the 12 muffin spots in the pan. Add crumb topping to each before baking.
- Bake for 18–22 minutes until a toothpick comes out clean after poking the middle. Remove from pan and cool on a rack.

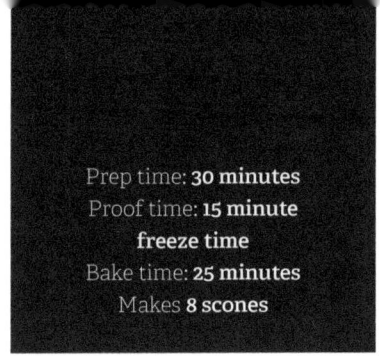

Prep time: **30 minutes**
Proof time: **15 minute freeze time**
Bake time: **25 minutes**
Makes **8 scones**

CHOCOLATE CHERRY ALMOND SCONES

2 cups all-purpose flour
½ cup sugar
2 teaspoons baking powder
½ teaspoon salt
1 cup bittersweet chocolate chips
½ cup dried cherries
½ cup slivered almonds
½ cup unsalted butter, FROZEN
½ cup heavy whipping cream, cold
1 egg
2 teaspoons pure vanilla extract

These scones are really a blank slate to do whatever you'd like, sconewise. Replace the chocolate, cherries, and almonds with just about any fresh or dried fruit or nuts. You can also go savory by reducing the sugar to 2 tablespoons and then adding grated cheese, nuts, or herbs.

- Preheat oven to 400°F.
- In one bowl, mix together the flour, sugar, baking powder and salt. Stir in the chocolate chips, dried cherries, and almonds. In separate bowl, whisk together the egg, cream, and vanilla. With a cheese grater, grate the frozen butter right into the flour mix. Pour the egg and cream mixture into the flour mix and gently stir until all incorporated, trying not to overmix.
- Dump out on a board and work the dough into a flat round disk about 8 inches across. With a knife or dough cutter, cut into eight wedges. Place them on a plate and put in freezer for 15–20 minutes, or ideally put them in the fridge overnight and bake the next morning.
- Remove from plate and place on parchment-lined baking sheet. Brush tops with a little cream and sprinkle with sugar. Bake for about 25 minutes. Let cool.

Prep time: **30 minutes**
Proof time: **about 2 hours**
Bake time: **30 minutes**
Makes **1 loaf**

JAPANESE MILK BREAD

TANGZHONG

⅓ cup all-purpose flour

½ cup milk

½ cup water

DOUGH

2½ cups all-purpose flour

¼ cup sugar

2¼ teaspoons active dry yeast

1 tablespoon nonfat dry milk powder

1 teaspoon salt

1 egg

½ cup milk, warmed

¼ cup unsalted butter, softened

heavy cream or milk to brush on top

This is the softest, fluffiest loaf of bread ever. There's an extra step here for creating a tangzhong, which is like a roux or paste that gelatinizes the flour, which then makes the bread super soft. Use this bread for sandwiches or make the best cinnamon toast you've ever had.

- First, make the tangzhong by heating a small saucepan with the ⅓ cup flour, ½ cup milk, and ½ cup water. Stir constantly until the mixture gums up and becomes a paste. Turn off heat and let this cool for about 15 minutes.
- In a stand mixer, combine the dry ingredients, then slowly add in the egg, ½ cup milk, and the tangzhong. Mix with a dough hook on medium speed for about 5 minutes. It will look dry and like it's not going to come together for a bit, but it will. After about 5 minutes, toss in the butter a little at a time, so it gets incorporated into the dough. Keep mixing for about 8 more minutes until the dough is soft and smooth.
- Remove from the mixer, cover the dough with a towel, and let rise for about an hour until doubled in size.
- Grease a nine-by-four-inch bread pan with butter and set aside.
- After an hour, place the dough on a lightly floured cutting board, and divide the dough into four equal parts. One at a time, roll out a dough portion so it's about five inches wide and eight inches long. Fold the long sides in so it's now about eight inches long and three inches wide, then roll it up into a burrito shape. Place seam side down in pan, then do the rest the same way, so you have four little burritos tucked into the loaf pan. Cover and let rise for about an hour.
- Preheat oven to 350°F. After second rise, brush the top with heavy cream or milk, then bake in the oven for about 30 minutes until the top is golden brown. When done, remove from oven and let sit in pan for about 5 more minutes. Remove and let cool before slicing.

Prep time: **30 minutes**
Proof time: **about 2 hours**
Bake time: **25–28 minutes**
Makes **9 rolls**

HOKKAIDO MILK ROLLS

TANGZHONG

2 tablespoons all-purpose flour
2 tablespoons water
4 tablespoons milk

DOUGH

2½ cups all-purpose flour
1 tablespoon active dry yeast
1 teaspoon salt
½ cup milk, warmed
¼ cup sugar
1 egg
3 tablespoons unsalted butter, softened

EGG WASH

1 egg yolk
1 tablespoon milk

These are perfect for a grand holiday meal, but equally great for just a normal Tuesday dinner. These buns can make a showstopping side that'll take down any Christmas ham or Thanksgiving turkey, but also makes a perfect little ham sandwich or accompaniment to a can of tomato soup.

Like the Japanese Milk Bread (see page 42), this recipe uses a tangzhong, which is essentially a mash of flour, water, and milk that gives these rolls a nice, fluffy texture.

MAKE THE TANGZHONG (THIS IS WHAT MAKES THEM SO GOOD!)

- In a small pot on the stove, on medium heat, combine the flour, water, and milk, and stir constantly. After a few minutes, the mix will suddenly seize up into a paste. Turn off heat and let cool for a bit.

MAKE THE DOUGH

- In a standing mixer fitted with a dough hook, mix the flour, yeast, salt, warm milk, sugar, and the egg. While it's mixing, add in the tangzhong paste, and then add the soft butter a bit at a time. Once it's all incorporated, mix for about 5 minutes until a ball forms. Transfer the ball to a slightly oiled bowl and cover. Set aside for about 1 hour or until doubled in size.
- Once doubled, divide the dough into nine even-size lumps on a cutting board. Roll each into a ball and place in a square pan that has been oiled with butter or oil. Make sure the top of each ball is smooth and any seams face down! Cover and let rise again for about an hour.
- Preheat oven to 350°F. Once the rolls have doubled in size, brush with the egg wash. Bake for about 25–28 minutes, rotating the pan about halfway through. Remove when golden brown.
- For an added bonus, brush with melted butter and sprinkle with flaky sea salt right after you take them out of the oven.

Prep time: **20 minutes**
Proof time: **about 2½ hours**
Bake time: **15 minutes**
Makes **16 rolls**

SEÑORITA BREAD

DOUGH

2 teaspoons active dry yeast
¼ cup water, warmed
1 teaspoon sugar
3½ cups all-purpose flour
½ cup sugar
1 teaspoon salt
½ cup milk
½ cup unsalted butter, melted
2 eggs

FOR THE FILLING

¼ cup unsalted butter, melted
½ cup breadcrumbs
½ cup sugar
2 tablespoons cinnamon
additional 1 tablespoon melted butter for brushing dough

These tasty little rolls are like a perfect combination of a croissant, a donut, and a dinner roll. Sweet, but not too sweet, perfect for dunking in coffee or eating all 16 at once.

- Proof the yeast by sprinkling the yeast over the warm water, giving it a quick stir. Let sit for about 5 to 10 minutes until it's foamy and frothy on top.
- In a large bowl, whisk together the flour, sugar, and salt, then add the milk, melted butter, eggs, and yeast, and combine. In a mixer with a dough hook, mix the dough until it comes together into a smooth ball. You can knead it with your hands, too, but will take a while longer.
- Lightly grease a bowl, place dough in bowl, cover with a towel, and let rise in a warm place until it doubles, about 2 hours.
- On a cutting board, divide the dough into two equal pieces. Form the two pieces into logs, then cut each log into eight equal-sized pieces. One at a time, take a piece and roll out into a three-by-five-inch rectangle. Brush the top with a little melted butter, then sprinkle with a little of the breadcrumb sugar cinnamon mix. Starting at one corner, roll up the dough with the mix on the inside.
- Transfer each to a parchment-lined cookie sheet. Brush the tops with a little more butter, then sprinkle a little more breadcrumb mix on top.
- Cover the rolls with a towel and let rise for another 30 minutes.
- Preheat the oven to 375°F. Bake for about 15 minutes until golden brown.

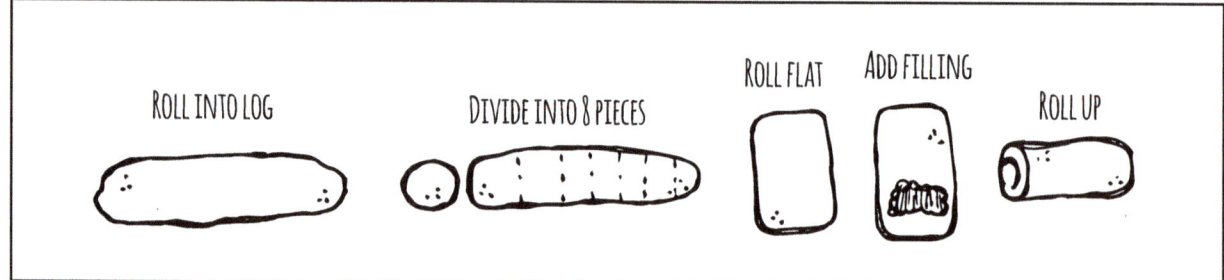

Roll into log · Divide into 8 pieces · Roll flat · Add filling · Roll up

Prep time: 20 minutes
Proof time: zero;
it's a quick bread
Bake time: 45 minutes
Makes 3 can size loaves

TIN CAN BREAD

3 empty bean cans (15 ounce)
1 cup raisins
1 teaspoon baking soda
1 cup water, hot
2 tablespoons unsalted butter, softened
1 cup sugar
1 teaspoon salt
1 teaspoon vanilla
1 egg
2 cups all-purpose flour
1 cup chopped peanuts, walnuts or pecans

I remember as a kid seeing bread baked in cans sold at our church bazaar. I don't remember actually eating it, just how cool they looked, kind of like the canned cranberry sauce at Thanksgiving. These are essentially just slightly dense muffins baked in a fun shape.

- Place the raisins and baking soda in a bowl and pour in the hot water. Let sit for a few minutes to soften up the raisins.
- In a bowl, whip together the butter and sugar into a crumbly mixture, either with a mixer or by hand. Add in all the other ingredients and mix into a batter.
- Generously coat the insides of 3 clean bean or soup cans with butter or oil, CAREFUL not to cut yourself if the edges are jagged. I use spray oil for this, to get all the way in there.
- Preheat the oven to 325°F. Fill the cans ¾ the way full. Place on a baking sheet, then top with a second baking sheet to form a lid. Bake for 45 minutes. Remove from oven, let cool, and if the stars are all aligned, the bread should slide right out. If not, use a knife to loosen the sides, then slide out.
- Slice into rounds and serve with butter or cream cheese.

Prep time: **5 minutes**
Proof time: **15 minutes**
Bake time: **4 minutes each**
Makes **6 flatbreads**

QUICK AND EASY FLATBREADS

2 cups all-purpose flour
1½ teaspoons baking powder
1 teaspoon salt
1 teaspoon sugar
2 tablespoons olive oil
¾ cup cold water
olive oil for cooking

During the first few months of the COVID lockdown, people turned to baking as a way to find comfort and pass the time while being cooped up inside. The problem was that flour was suddenly hard to find. If you found flour, the next challenge was finding yeast. Sourdough boomed in popularity because you made your own yeast, but sourdough is a long process and hard to master. Luckily, yeast isn't the only way to make bread rise. Here, we use baking powder to give the dough a boost. And these flatbreads are ready in about a half hour, start to finish!

- In a bowl, mix together the flour, baking powder, sugar, and salt. Pour in the olive oil and water and mix together with a spoon until incorporated. Turn out onto a cutting board and knead it about 6–8 times until you have a smooth ball of dough. Place back in the bowl and let rest for about 10 minutes.
- After 10 minutes, divide the dough into six pieces and roll them into balls. With a rolling pin, roll them out into ¼-inch thick disks.
- Heat a little oil in a frying pan over medium heat, and one at a time, cook the bread for about 2 minutes, flip, then cook the other side for about 2 minutes until golden brown. Repeat with the rest.
- Keep them warm by wrapping in a dish towel while making the rest.
- Brush with melted butter and garlic if you choose, or just eat as is!

PART 4
RISE UP!

EASY RECIPES THAT TAKE A BIT MORE TIME AND EFFORT

NO-KNEAD ARTISAN CHEDDAR JALAPEÑO BREAD

Prep time: **10 minutes**
Proof time: **7 hours**
Bake time: **45 minutes**
Makes **1 loaf**

3 cups all-purpose flour
2 teaspoons salt
1 teaspoon active dry yeast
1½ cups warm water
½ cup shredded cheddar cheese
¼ cup chopped pickled jalapeños

No-knead bread is a great introduction to artisan bread baking. This will get you ready to take on sourdough in the next chapter. Make sure you start this early in the day as it needs seven hours to proof! The cheese and jalapeños add a ton of flavor to this, but if you don't want it, just leave that out.

- In a big bowl, mix all the ingredients, the flour, salt, dry yeast, warm water, shredded cheddar cheese, and chopped jalapeños, into a shaggy ball, making sure there's no dry flour left. Cover with a towel and let sit to rise for six hours. Dump the dough onto a floured board. Flatten out a bit, then fold the dough over on itself. Keep folding until it becomes a round, tight ball. Place the seam down and put on a piece of parchment paper. Cover with a towel and let rise for another hour.
- Preheat oven to 450°F with a Dutch oven and lid in the oven. Once oven is heated, carefully remove the Dutch oven. Lift the parchment with the dough and set it inside the Dutch oven. Give the top a few quick slashes with a knife or razorblade. Place the lid back on and bake for 30 minutes. After 30, remove the lid and bake another 15 minutes until golden brown.
- Remove from Dutch oven and let cool for about a half hour before slicing.

NO-KNEAD ARTISAN CHEDDAR JALAPEÑO BREAD

Prep time: **30 minutes**
Proof time: **4–5 hours** (plus overnight rise for the starter)
Bake time: **40 minutes**
Makes 1 loaf

GREEN ONION PULLMAN BREAD

NOTE

You will need a Pullman loaf pan with a lid to make this loaf. You can use a regular bread loaf pan, but then the loaf won't come out a rectangle.

STARTER

¼ cup all-purpose flour
a pinch of active dry yeast
a pinch of salt
1 teaspoon sugar
3 tablespoons cold milk

DOUGH

3½ cups all-purpose flour
¼ cup sugar
1 teaspoon salt
2 teaspoons active dry yeast
1¼ cups cold milk
3 eggs
8 tablespoons unsalted butter, softened
1 cup thinly chopped green onions

Pullman loaves are long, perfectly rectangular loaves. They were originally used on train dining cars so the bakers could cram more loaves into the small ovens by stacking the closed lid pans. This recipe is also great without the onions. If you want a more traditional loaf, just leave them out.

MAKE THE STARTER

- The night before, in a small bowl, mix the starter ingredients into a paste. Cover with a towel and leave on the counter. In the morning, it'll be puffy and ready to go!

MAKE THE BREAD

- In a large bowl, add the milk, then add the puffy starter to it. With your fingers, break apart the starter as best you can. Add in the flour, salt, yeast, green onions, and eggs. Stir with your hand (it works best!) or a big spoon until it all comes together. It'll be very sticky.
- Sprinkle some flour on a board and scrape the dough onto the floured surface. Knead the dough for about 5 minutes until it starts getting smoother and stops sticking to everything. Form it into a ball, cover with a towel, and let it sit for about 15 minutes.
- On same lightly floured surface, take the ball and gently stretch it out into a big rectangle shape (about twelve by ten inches). Frost the surface of the dough with 7 tablespoons of butter. It doesn't have to cover it all and doesn't need to look pretty. Fold the dough up like a letter so the butter is now inside the dough, with one third folding in, then the other side folding over that folded part. Now take the opposite ends and fold them up so you roughly have a ball again. Place the ball back in the bowl and cover with a towel. Let rise for 45–60 minutes.
- On same lightly floured surface, take the ball and gently stretch it out again. Refold it the same way you did the first time. Place the ball back in the bowl and cover with a towel. Let rise for 45–60 minutes.
- Okay, once more. On same lightly floured surface, take the ball and gently stretch it out again. Refold it the same way you did the first time. Place the ball back in the bowl and cover with a towel. Let rise for 45–60 minutes.
- Generously butter the insides of the loaf pan.
- Dust your work surface one last time and do one more stretching out. Fold it again like a letter, but this time, fold it again so it roughly matches the size of the pan. Carefully lift it and place into buttered pan, seam side down.

Make sure the edges are all tucked down. Spread a little more butter on top and slide the lid on.
- Your final rise can be anywhere from 2-4 hours. Keep an eye on it. When the dough is about a half-inch from the lid, you are ready to go.
- Preheat the oven to 375°F.

NOTE: Place a rimmed baking sheet on the lower rack to catch any butter that drips out or you'll set off your smoke detectors. Trust me on this. Sometimes, parts of the dough will squeeze out of the corners of the pan and make curly breadsticks to munch on. The baking sheet will catch these, too.

- Bake the loaf for 30 minutes with the lid on, rotating the pan halfway through.
- Remove from oven, take the loaf out of the pan (careful, it's hot!) and return the loaf to the oven, right on the rack, for an additional 8-10 minutes.
- Let cool before slicing.

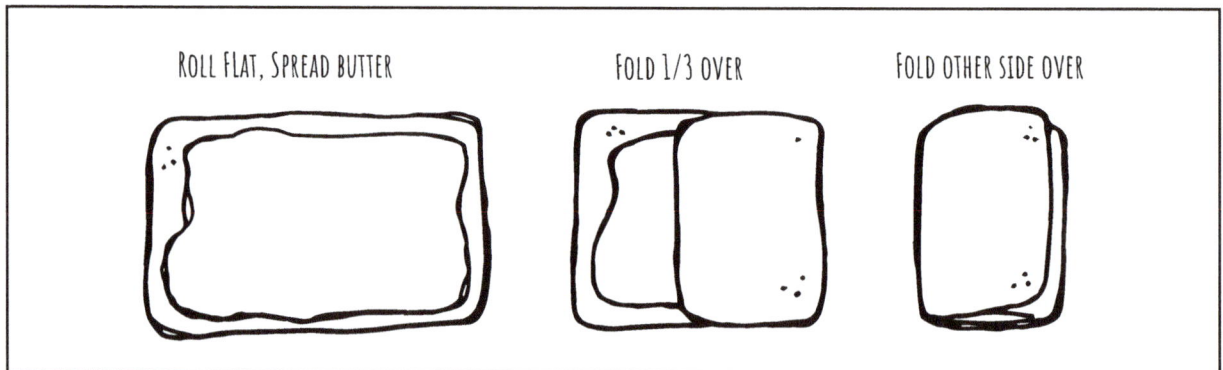

GREEN ONION PULLMAN BREAD

Prep time: **30 minutes**
Proof time: **18 or so hours**
Bake time: **8 minutes**
Makes **6 pizza doughs**

PERFECT PIZZA CRUST

8 cups all-purpose flour
3¼ cups water, warmed
1 tablespoon sea salt
¼ teaspoon active dry yeast

Plan ahead because this pizza dough isn't for tonight. It's for tomorrow night, but it's well worth the wait! For pizza on Friday night, start this Thursday night. It makes 6 pizzas, so your patience will pay off in pies all weekend long. The fresh doughs will keep for about 4 days, and they get better and better as the days pass.

- In a small bowl, mix the warm water with the yeast and set aside.
- In a large bowl, mix the flour and salt, then pour in the water yeast mix. Mix by hand until all the flour is wet and incorporated. Let sit for about 20 minutes.
- Reach under the dough mix and pull up, so you are pulling the dough up and over itself. Do this a few times. Cover and let rest for 30 minutes.
- After 30 minutes, do this stretch and fold technique again a few times. Cover and let rest for another 30 minutes. Do the stretch and fold one more time (a total of 3 times), then lightly oil the top of the dough, cover with a towel, and let sit out on counter overnight (about 12–14 hours).
- In the morning, dump the dough out on a floured cutting board. Shape it into a ball, then with a dough cutter, try to cut into six equal parts. Doesn't need to be exact. Carefully roll each piece into a ball, folding the dough in on itself so there is some surface tension on the top side. Set them seams down on a floured baking sheet. Do this to all six portions.
- Lightly oil the tops, then cover with a towel and place in refrigerator for 4–6 more hours.
- See page 150 for pizza making and baking recipes!
- Unused doughs can be placed in individual plastic containers or plastic bags and refrigerated for up to 4 days or frozen for a few months.

Prep time: **30 minutes**
Proof time: **3–4 hours**
Bake time: **30 minutes**
Makes **1 loaf**

CHALLAH

1 cup water, warm
2 teaspoons active dry yeast
4¼ cups all-purpose flour
2 teaspoons salt
¼ cup sugar
¼ cup vegetable oil
2 eggs
1 more egg for wash

Challah is a brioche-style bread braided into a beautiful loaf. It looks way more difficult than it really is, you just need to pay attention and brush up on your braiding skills. This makes excellent French toast, by the way.

- In a small bowl, mix together the warm water, yeast, and a pinch of the sugar. Let sit until foamy, about 5–10 minutes. In the bowl of your mixer, add the flour, salt, and sugar and mix. With the dough hook on medium, slowly add in the yeast mixture, the oil, and both eggs. Continue mixing until the dough starts forming a ball in around the hook but is still clinging to the bottom of the bowl, about 7–8 minutes.
- Scrape the sticky dough out onto a floured cutting board and knead a few times, then form into a tight ball. Place in an oiled bowl, swirling it so the top of the dough is also oiled. Cover with a towel and let rise until doubled in size, about 2 hours.
- Move dough back onto a floured cutting board and divide the dough into four equal pieces. Stretch and roll them into four twelve- to fourteen-inch-long snakes, and line them up next to each other on a parchment-lined baking sheet. Pinch together the far ends, then fan out the other ends in order to easily braid them.
- To braid, take the snake on the far right, and weave to the left, going over, under, over. Now do it again with the new farthest right snake, over, under, over. Repeat until it's all braided, then tuck the ends under the loaf. Loosely cover with a towel and let rise for about another 1–2 hours.
- Preheat oven to 350°F. Make an egg wash by beating the last egg, then gently brushing the egg over the dough. Bake in oven for about 30 minutes until golden brown. Let cool before slicing.

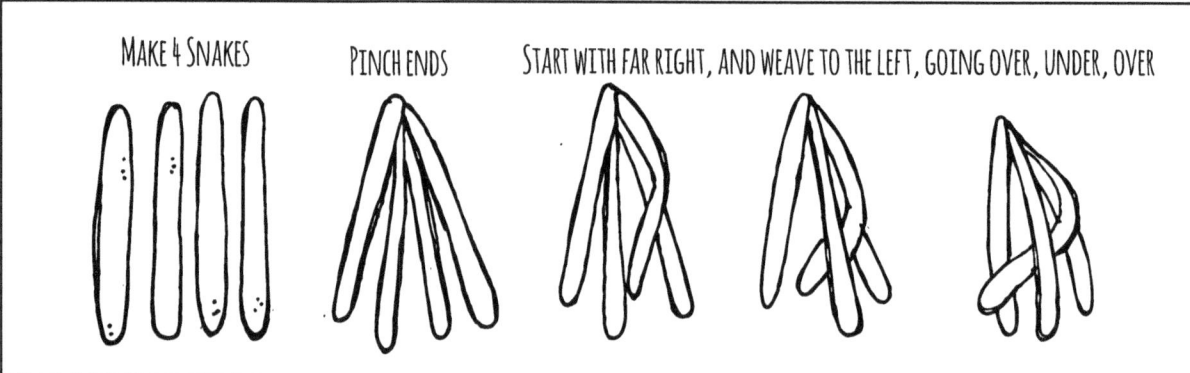

Prep time: **1 hour**
Proof time: **about 1½ hours,** PLUS overnight if you want
Cook time: **3–4 minutes**
Makes **1 dozen donuts plus a bunch of holes**

BLUEBERRY DONUTS

Making donuts at home is a dangerous game. Once you realize that you can have piping hot donuts any morning of the week, you'll be hooked. If you don't want to do the blueberries, just leave them out. You can also make powdered donuts by dropping the hot donuts into a brown paper bag with powdered sugar or a sugar cinnamon mix and give it a shake-shake.

DOUGH

2¼ teaspoons active dry yeast
1¼ cups milk, warmed
½ cup sugar
1 teaspoon salt
2 eggs
1 cup unsalted butter, melted
4 cups all-purpose flour
½ cup fresh or frozen blueberries, blended or squashed up
2 quarts vegetable oil for frying

ICING

½ cup butter, melted
2 teaspoons vanilla
4 cups powdered sugar
small amount of additional water if it's too thick

- In the bowl of your mixer, add the warm milk, sugar, and yeast, stir to combine, then let sit for about 5 minutes until foamy on top. Add in melted butter, blueberries, and eggs, then whisk to combine. With mixer on, slowly add the flour and salt. Mix with a dough hook for about 5 minutes until dough comes together in a smooth ball. Place dough in lightly oiled fresh bowl, cover the top of the dough with plastic wrap, then place in refrigerator for 2 hours.

NOTE: You can do this the night before, then just place the dough in the fridge until the next morning. This is the ideal way to go!

- Place your cold dough on a lightly floured cutting board and roll out the dough to be about a ½-inch thick. With ring cutters, cut out the donuts and holes and place on a parchment paper on a baking sheet. Cover with a towel and let rise until very poofy, about an hour or two.
- Heat a few inches of oil in a pan until the oil is about 350°F. Add the dough and fry a few at a time until they are golden brown. I use chopsticks to flip them and keep from sticking to each other. Chopsticks are also great for pulling them out of the oil, but a slotted spoon works great, too. The donuts will take a few minutes, but the holes will cook superfast, like 30 seconds. Drain on paper towels, then dip in glaze or put them in a paper bag filled with powdered sugar and give a shake-shake!
- For glaze, mix the butter, vanilla, and powdered sugar in a bowl. It'll be thick, then start to thin it out by adding a little water until you have a consistency to dip into.
- Eat them now; don't wait.

Prep time: **25 minutes**
Proof time: **1½ hours**
Bake time: **40 minutes**
Makes **2 loaves**

BLUEBERRY CREAM CHEESE BABKA

Babkas are beautiful loaves of bread that are sort of like a brioche bread braided with a filling, usually chocolate, but here I used a mix of blueberries and cream cheese. Braiding the unbaked dough is a bit of a challenge. You'll definitely get blueberries on you if you wear white.

DOUGH

4 cups all-purpose flour
4 teaspoons active dry yeast
½ cup sugar
1 cup warm milk
½ cup unsalted butter, melted
3 eggs
1 teaspoon vanilla
1 teaspoon salt

BLUEBERRY FILLING

2 cups fresh or frozen blueberries
½ cup sugar
¼ cup corn starch
8 oz. softened cream cheese

CRUMB TOPPING

¼ cup flour
½ cup sugar
1 tablespoon cinnamon
2 tablespoons melted butter

- In the bowl of a stand mixer with a dough hook, mix the flour, yeast, sugar, and salt. With the mixer on, slowly pour in the milk, add the eggs, then pour in the melted butter. Mix on medium speed for about 10 minutes until dough starts to pull away from the sides. It'll be smooth and shiny. After 10 minutes, remove the hook, cover, and let sit to rise for about a ½ hour.
- In the meantime, make the blueberry filling. In a saucepan, heat the berries, sugar, and corn starch for a few minutes. Either mash them with a fork or blend with a stick blender. Remove from heat, then add in the cream cheese. Mix together as the berries cool and the cream cheese softens. This should be the consistency of peanut butter.
- Take two nine-by-four-inch bread pans, spray with oil, then lay in a piece of parchment paper, too.
- On a floured cutting board, divide the dough in half and put one half off to the side. Gently stretch the dough into a larger rectangle, about twelve by fourteen inches. With a spoon, spread half the blueberry mixture onto the dough, leaving about an inch all around the edges blank. Starting at the shorter end, tightly roll the dough up into a tube. Here's where it gets tricky. Now take that tube and cut it down the middle lengthwise.
- Pinch the back ends together, then carefully braid the two lines of dough, one side over the next. You should now have a very messy, braided dough with blueberry gunk all over. Good job! Now, carefully lift this into the prepared pan. Now go wash your hands, and repeat it with the second loaf or make a different filling for the next one. Chocolate babka is the real deal.
- Cover the loaves and let rise for about an hour.
- Preheat oven to 350°F. Brush the tops of the loaves with a little milk, then sprinkle the crumb topping on. Bake for about 40 minutes. Let cool, then slice.

BREAD BAKING BASICS

BLUEBERRY CREAM CHEESE BABKA

CROISSANTS TWO WAYS

Prep time: **about an hour**
Proof time: **Beware, this is a three-day process! But well worth it.**
Bake time: **13–15 minutes**
Makes **16 rectangles** or **24 croissants**

This is definitely a time commitment, but you don't win a marathon by just running one day. And you don't get buttery, flakey chocolate croissants by just snapping your fingers. It's a three-day process, but only a little time each day. I like to make half of them sweet and half savory, or some just plain. On day three, you can choose which way you want to go and branch off from this core recipe.

DOUGH

1½ cups water
¼ cup sugar
4½ cups all-purpose flour
2½ teaspoons active dry yeast
2½ teaspoons salt
4 tablespoons unsalted butter, room temperature

BUTTER FILLING

1½ cups (24 tablespoons) cold, unsalted butter
1 tablespoon flour

EGG WASH

1 egg
pinch of salt

DAY 1

- In your mixing bowl, combine the water, sugar, 3 cups of flour, the yeast, salt, and the 4 tablespoons of butter, and mix with the dough hook. With the mixer running, slowing add in the additional 1½ cups of flour. You may not need it all, so add a little at a time and stop when the dough starts pulling away from the sides. Once it starts pulling away, mix for about 3 more minutes.
- Oil a new bowl, place the dough in it, swirl it around so it's all oiled, cover, and let rise for about an hour. After an hour or so, cover the surface of the oiled dough with plastic wrap, then place a towel over the whole thing and put in the fridge overnight (up to 24 hours).

DAY 2

- The next step is getting the butter between all the layers of dough. Start by taking a piece of parchment and sprinkle with half a tablespoon of flour. Take your 3 sticks of butter and slice them lengthwise and lay them flat on the flour. Sprinkle the other half tablespoon of flour over the top, then lay a second sheet of parchment over the top. With a rolling pin, start whacking the heck out of the butter! We are working the flour into the butter and making it all a little more flexible. Peel back the parchment, and fold the butter up on itself, then cover and whack some more. Do this a few times, finally rolling the butter into an eight-inch square.
- Now get your dough out of the fridge, and on a floured surface roll it out into fourteen-inch circle. Place the butter square in the middle, then fold the sides up and over, completely enclosing the butter like a Hot Pocket.
- Take your butter packet, and roll it out into a big rectangle, then fold it up in thirds, like a letter. Repeat this process, rolling it back out then folding up. Wrap it up in plastic wrap and put in the fridge to rest for about 2 hours.
- Remove from the fridge, and repeat the rolling out into a rectangle, then return to the folding like a letter process. Now do it one more time (for a total of 4 roll out/fold ups). Wrap it up in plastic wrap and put in the fridge to rest overnight.

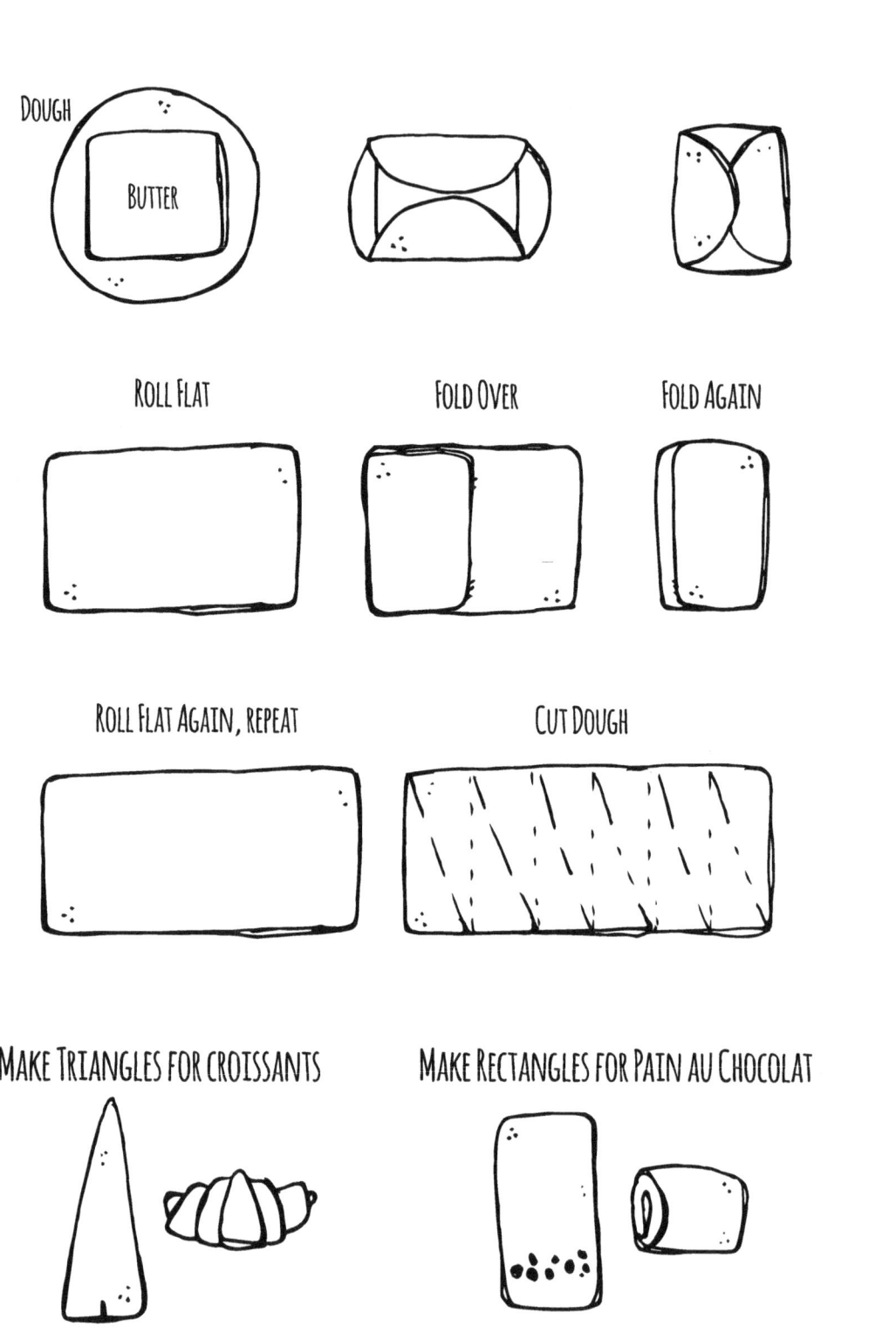

DAY 3

- Remove your dough from the fridge. Prepare 3 baking sheets with parchment paper. Cut the dough in half. Take one half and roll out into a large rectangle. Decide if you want to make rectangular shapes or croissant shapes.
- For rectangles, roll the dough to be roughly eight by twenty-four inches, then cut that into 8 four-by-six-inch rectangles. Add a filling (see following pages) and roll into a tube. Place seam side down on the parchment.
- For croissants, roll out into an eight-by-twenty-four-inch rectangle, then cut into six four-by-eight-inch rectangles, then cut each of those diagonally so you have 12 triangles. Cut a small slit in the dough on the end opposite from the point, then roll up to the point is on the outside. Move to prepared sheets.
- Let these rise for about an hour. Preheat oven to 425°F. Beat the egg with the pinch of salt and brush the tops of the dough. Bake for about 15 minutes until golden brown.

Makes **8 Pain au Chocolat**

PAIN AU CHOCOLAT

1 cup of semi-sweet chocolate (chips or bars)

half of the croissant dough recipe (see page 71)

- When you get to the final roll-out part, place about a tablespoon of chocolate bits on one end of the dough rectangle, then start rolling, then add a few more pieces of chocolate, so when baked, the chocolate will be in more than one area.
- Let them rise for about an hour. Preheat oven to 425°F. Beat the egg with the pinch of salt and brush the tops of the dough. Bake for about 15 minutes until golden brown.

HAM AND SWISS CROISSANTS WITH THYME

12 small strips of Swiss cheese
12 pieces of sliced ham
1 tablespoon chopped fresh thyme
half of the croissant dough recipe
   (see page 71)
cracked pepper
3 tablespoons Dijon mustard
3 tablespoons honey

- When you get to the final roll-out part, place a piece of cheese and ham on the bottom part of the tringle, then roll ham and cheese up in the croissant.
- Let them rise for about an hour. Preheat oven to 425°F. Beat the egg with the pinch of salt and brush the tops of the dough, then sprinkle the tops with thyme and cracked pepper. Bake for about 15 minutes until golden brown.
- While baking, stir together the honey and mustard and serve with the finished croissants.

BUTTERMILK CINNAMON ROLLS WITH CINNAMON ICING

Prep time: **25 minutes**
Proof time: **1½ hours**
Bake time: **40 minutes**
Makes **9 rolls**

What is better when you wake up in the morning than the smell of fresh-baked cinnamon rolls? The problem here is if it's you baking, you'll not be the one walking up to the smell. But that's a small problem, soon to be fixed with the smell of cinnamon rolls.

DOUGH

4 cups all-purpose flour
3 teaspoons active dry yeast
½ cup sugar
1 cup buttermilk, warm
½ cup unsalted butter, melted then cooled
2 eggs
1 teaspoon vanilla
1 teaspoon salt

FILLING

½ cup unsalted butter, melted
1 cup brown sugar
2 tablespoons cinnamon

ICING

8 oz. cream cheese (one box)
¼ cup unsalted butter, room temperature
2 cups powdered sugar
½ tablespoon vanilla
1 tablespoon cinnamon

- In the bowl of a stand mixer with a dough hook, mix the flour, yeast, sugar, and salt. With the mixer on, slowly pour in the buttermilk, add the eggs, then pour in the melted butter. Mix on medium speed for about 10 minutes until dough starts to pull away from the sides. It'll be smooth and shiny. After 10 minutes, remove the hook, cover, and let sit to rise for about a half hour.
- While dough is rising, make the filling. Just mix all the filling ingredients together in a bowl, then set aside.
- When dough has doubled, dump it out onto a well-floured cutting board. Roll out the dough so it's about twenty-four by sixteen inches. With a spatula, smear the cinnamon filling over the dough so it completely covers the dough. Starting on one of the long sides, carefully roll the dough into a long tube like you are rolling up a carpet. Cut the dough into nine hockey pucks and place into a greased nine-by-thirteen-inch baking pan. Cover and let rise for about a half hour.
- Preheat oven to 375°F. Bake for about 20 minutes until the tops are nice and brown. Remove from oven and let cool. While cooling, in a mixer or by hand, beat together all the icing ingredients, then spread evenly over the rolls.

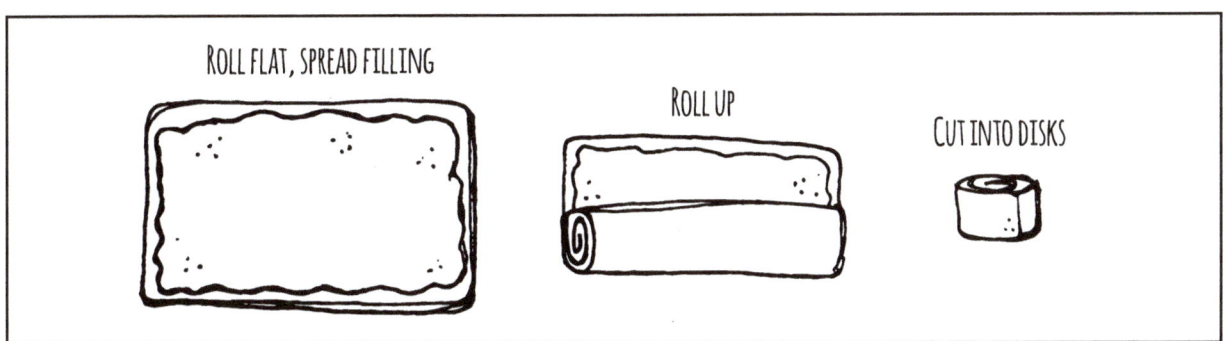

Prep time: **30 minutes**
Proof time: **about 2½ hours**
Bake time: **15–18 minutes**
Makes **12 conchas**

CONCHAS

Conchas are type of Mexican sweet breads, also called Pan Dulce. Soft and fluffy with a sweet crunchy top, these have become an all-around favorite at our house.

DOUGH

2 teaspoons active dry yeast
½ cup water, warmed
½ cup milk, warmed
⅓ cup sugar
4 tablespoons unsalted butter, melted
1 egg
1 teaspoon salt
4 cups all-purpose flour
1 teaspoon cinnamon

TOPPING

⅔ cup sugar
½ cup unsalted butter, room temperature
1 cup all-purpose flour
½ teaspoon baking powder
1 teaspoon vanilla extract
1 tablespoon unsweetened cocoa powder

- In a small bowl, mix the yeast and warm water. Set it aside for a few minutes.
- In the mixer bowl, stir the milk, sugar, melted butter, egg, salt, and cinnamon with 2 cups of the flour. Mix with the dough hook for about 3 minutes, then start slowly adding the additional 2 cups of flour. Mix with dough hook until the dough starts pulling away from the sides and forms a ball. Move the dough to an oiled bowl, then cover with a towel for about 1 hour or until its doubled in size.
- Divide the dough into twelve pieces. Do your best to roll each piece into a smooth ball. It helps to kind of fold the dough over itself to make the top side of the bun a tight, smooth surface. Make sure you place it seam side down on the parchment.
- Place buns onto two parchment-lined baking sheets, six per sheet.
- To make the topper, add the softened butter and sugar to a mixing bowl and beat for a minute. Add in the flour, vanilla, and baking powder and beat until it forms a paste, adding a tiny bit of water if it's not coming together. If you want to make some of the conchas brown, divide the mixture in half, and in a second bowl, mix in the cocoa powder.
- Now divide the paste into twelve equal-size pieces (they will be pretty small). Roll each into a ball, then flatten it between your palms so it's about three inches across and pretty thin. Carefully drape a disk over the top of each dough ball. With a sharp knife (or you can buy concha pattern molds, too) cut into the dough to make shapes. You can crisscross or make lines that look like the top of a shell.
- Lightly cover and let rise for about 1½ hours or until very puffy.
- Preheat oven to 350°F. Bake in oven for about 15–18 minutes.

LEMON, ROSEMARY, TOMATO FOCACCIA

1 teaspoon active dry yeast
2 teaspoons sugar
1 cup warm water
⅛ cup olive oil
2¼ cups all-purpose flour
1 tablespoon salt
2 tablespoons chopped rosemary
1 tablespoon lemon zest (from 1 lemon)
2 additional tablespoons olive oil
handful of cherry tomatoes
flaky sea salt

Focaccia is one of the easiest breads to make, because there's really no shaping involved. You just plop it into a pan and stick your fingers all over it. Simple! This recipe is best if you put it in the fridge overnight to help develop the flavors. You can leave out the lemon and rosemary and just make focaccia-flavored focaccia. It's also very trendy right now to make a flower design on top with veggie parts. Do that if you must, but this tomato top is equally beautiful and delicious.

- In a large bowl, mix together the yeast, sugar, and ⅛ cup olive oil, then pour in the warm water and let sit for a few minutes. Add in the flour, salt, rosemary, and lemon zest.
- Using your hands or a wooden spoon, mix until all the flour is wet. Form the sticky dough into a ball, then cover the bowl with a towel or plastic wrap. Let rise for about 2–3 hours on the countertop, until doubled in size.
- Generously oil a nine-inch pie pan or an iron skillet with 1 tablespoon oil. Punch down the dough and, with your hands, form it into a disk about the size of the pan you are using. Try to keep the thickness pretty even. This doesn't need to be exact. Place in the pan to get oil all over the bottom of the dough, then flip the dough so both sides get nice and oily. Place plastic wrap directly over the dough and put in the fridge for at least 10 hours and up to a few days. If you leave for more than a day, make sure the plastic wrap is right on top of the dough to keep from drying out.

NEXT DAY

- Preheat oven to 425°F.
- Take out of fridge and let it warm up to room temperature for 2 hours. Dough should be puffy. Take the cherry tomatoes and push them down into the dough about halfway. With your fingers, poke dimples into the dough where you don't already have tomatoes. Drizzle the remaining tablespoon of oil over the top. Sprinkle the top with flaky sea salt, toss in oven, and bake for 20–25 minutes.

CANDIED ORANGE PRETZELED BAGELS

Prep time: 30 minutes
Proof time: 1 hour, plus overnight rest
Bake time: 22 minutes
Makes **8 bagels**

Bagels are fairly easy to make—you just need to master the technique of boiling the dough. You get pretty hot hovering over a pot of boiling water while the oven is on, so beware! These will come out of the oven looking really dark due to the baking soda in the boil. This is the same technique you use to make pretzels.

NOTE

You can leave out the orange to make plain bagels. You can also switch up what you top them with, too. Try Everything Bagel spice or sesame seeds.

DOUGH

1 tablespoon sugar
1 teaspoon active dry yeast
1½ teaspoons sea salt
1 cup plus 2 tablespoons warm water
3½ cups all-purpose flour
⅔ cup chopped candied orange peel (recipe on the next page)
2 tablespoons poppyseeds for topping

WATER BATH

2 quarts water
1½ tablespoons honey
1 tablespoon baking soda
1 teaspoon salt

- In a mixing bowl of the standing mixer, add all the dough ingredients (minus the poppyseeds). With the dough hook, mix on medium for about 3 minutes. Turn it off and let the dough sit for about 3 minutes, then turn back on and mix on medium again for about 3 more minutes. You should now have a smooth ball. Put dough into clean bowl, cover with a towel, and let rise in a nice, warm spot for about an hour.
- Line a baking sheet with parchment. On a cutting board, dump out the dough and divide into eight equal pieces. There are two ways to shape the bagel. One is to roll the dough into a snake, then connect the ends and roll those ends together with the palm of your hand. I find this way tends to make an uneven bagel unless you have a lot of practice. The pros use this technique, but I have an easier way. I tend to just roll the dough into a ball, then fold it in on itself until the top has a nice smooth surface, like we did with the buns. Then I just stick my finger right through it and wiggle it around until I have about a 2-inch hole. Works every time.
- Place the eight bagels on the baking sheet, spray or brush with a little oil, then cover with plastic wrap. Place in the refrigerator and let sit overnight.
- The next morning, preheat the oven to 450°F. In a big pot, bring the water bath ingredients to a boil. Drop the bagels into the water a few at a time. Let them boil for about 30 seconds, then flip them with a slotted spoon and boil the other side for 30 seconds. With the slotted spoon, fish the bagels out and place back on parchment-covered baking sheet. Repeat with all the bagels. Sprinkle with seeds if you like, or you can leave them plain.
- Bake in oven for about 15–18 minutes, rotating the sheet halfway through. Bagels are done when nice and brown. Place on wire rack to cool.
- To serve, toast 'em up and slather with cream cheese.

CANDIED ORANGE PEELS

3 large oranges
1 cup water
2 cups white sugar
additional sugar for dusting

- With a vegetable peeler, cut the skin off the oranges. Try to keep them in about inch-long pieces. Save the insides of the oranges to eat later. Place peels in a pot, then cover with water about an inch higher than the peels. Bring to a boil. Now, drain the peels, refill the pan, and bring to a second boil. This helps pull the bitterness out of the peels.
- In the same pan, mix 1 cup of water and the 2 cups of sugar. Heat until the sugar is dissolved, then add in the boiled peels. Cook the peels in the sugar syrup for about 45 minutes until the peels start looking translucent. Drain the peels again, toss with a little dry sugar, then lay on a drying rack. Let them dry for a few hours. Store in an airtight container.

CANDIED ORANGE PRETZELED BAGELS

PART 5
GLUTEN, OUT!

EASY RECIPES FOR A GLUTEN-FREE DIET

GLUTEN-FREE BAKING

I have to admit, being a flour loving baker, I've avoided the gluten-free baking trend for a long time. Partially, I've avoided it because if you are truly allergic to gluten, anything coming out of my kitchen most likely has some gluten in it, in small doses, because I live in a constant state of being partially covered in flour.

If you are truly allergic to gluten and want to learn more and perfect your gluten-free baking, I urge you to develop your own baking mix of flours. Common gluten-free flours are white rice flour, brown rice flour, tapioca flour, potato starch, quinoa flour, sorghum, coconut, almond, and corn. Most flour blends also have xanthan gum, guar gum, or a flax mix that act as binders.

I find that since I rarely bake gluten-free, it's easier and cheaper to just purchase premixed gluten-free flours. I've used Bob's Red Mill All-Purpose, Krusteaz Gluten-Free, and King Arthur Gluten-Free with great success. If you do plan to bake gluten-free more and more, research different blend ratios and make your own. Not all store-bought brands work the same, though. I've specified which brands work for my recipes. You may need to make adjustments if you are using a different brand or a home blend. Make sure you are getting the gluten-free all-purpose blends for baking breads, not the one-to-one blends.

Before COVID-19, it was super cheap to go to the bulk section of your grocery store and get just enough tapioca flour and brown rice flour, or whatever unique flours you were looking for, but as I write this, finding even regular flour is sometimes a challenge, let alone specialty flours and xanthan gums.

When baking with gluten-free flours, throw out the window a lot of the regular techniques you've been learning here. To get the shape you want, you need to kind of treat it like playdough. If you want an oval loaf, shape it like an oval. If you want a round, shape it in a ball. Pizza, you flatten it out into a circle.

Prep time: **10 minutes**
Proof time: **2½ hours**
Bake time: **25 minutes**
Makes **1 twelve-inch round**

GLUTEN-FREE FOCACCIA

Gluten-free focaccia is about as easy to make as anything in this book. Make a batter, oil the pan, scrape it in, and poke your fingers in it. That's about it! Quick and easy and pretty darn delicious. Remember, all gluten-free flours are a little different, so if you use one that's not listed, it may not exactly work.

DOUGH

3 cups gluten-free all-purpose flour (Bob's Red Mill or Krusteaz)
2 teaspoons active dry yeast
1 tablespoon sugar
2 teaspoons salt
2 cups milk, warm
4 tablespoons unsalted butter, melted

TOPPING

2 tablespoons olive oil
Maldon flake salt
fresh cracked pepper

- In a large bowl, combine all the dough ingredients. Whisk together until it forms a thick batter-like dough. Cover and let sit for about 2 hours. It'll rise a bit. After 2 hours, place in the refrigerator, covered, until you are ready to use. Do it for at least 2 hours, which will make the dough easier to handle. You can leave it for a few days.
- In a nine-inch cast-iron skillet or round pan, pour in 1 tablespoon of olive oil. Scrape out the dough onto the oil in the pan, then pour 1 more tablespoon over the top. Poke house about halfway into the dough all over, letting the holes fill with oil. Cover and let sit for about a half hour.
- Preheat the oven to 400°F, sprinkle the top with Maldon flake salt, cracked pepper and chopped rosemary, or whatever other toppings you'd like. Bake for about 25 minutes until golden brown.

Prep time: **10 minutes**
Proof time: **3 hours, plus at least 2 hours in refrigerator**
Bake time: **30 minutes**
Makes **4 pizzas**

GLUTEN-FREE PIZZA DOUGH

1 tablespoon active dry yeast
1½ cups water, warm
2 tablespoons olive oil
3 cups gluten-free all-purpose flour (Bob's Red Mill or Krusteaz)
1½ teaspoons xanthan gum
1 teaspoon salt
1 tablespoon sugar

This gluten-free pizza dough is fairly easy to do and becomes a nice vehicle to get pizza toppings into your mouth.

- Mix all ingredients in a bowl. Cover and let sit out on counter for 2 hours. After 2 hours, move to the refrigerator, and let cool for at least 2 more hours. The cold dough is much easier to shape than room temperature dough.
- Divide the dough into four equal-size balls. On a well-floured (rice flour) piece of parchment, gently roll out a ball, one at a time, into a ten- to twelve-inch round. Smooth out the edges with your hands and maybe a little water.
- Preheat oven to 500°F, with a pizza stone inside. Place the dough and parchment on a pizza peel, and then add your toppings. When the oven reaches 500°F, slide the pizza onto the stone (with the parchment) and bake for about 8 minutes. To remove, use your peel, and maybe kitchen tongs to help guide it out.

Prep time: **10 minutes**
Proof time: **6 hours**
Bake time: **60 minutes**
Makes **1 softball sized loaf**

GLUTEN-FREE ARTISAN LOAF

2 teaspoons active dry yeast
2 teaspoons sugar
1 cup water, warm
1½ cups all-purpose gluten-free flour (Bob's Red Mill or Krusteaz)
4 teaspoons xanthan gum
1 teaspoon salt
1 teaspoon baking powder
1 tablespoon chopped fresh rosemary
2 cloves of garlic, cut into chunks

This gluten-free loaf is fairly easy to make. It makes a pretty small loaf. There really isn't a technique involved in shaping. Because there are no glutens involved, there are no stretches and folds. It's really just like shaping a loaf out of playdough. Remember, all gluten-free flours are a little different, so if you use one that's not listed, it may not exactly work. Leave out the rosemary and garlic if you want.

- Mix the yeast, sugar, and water in a bowl and let sit for a few minutes until foamy.
- Add in the flour, xanthan gum, salt, baking powder, garlic, and rosemary. Mix well and let sit, covered, on the counter for at least 4 hours.
- Lay a piece of parchment on a baking sheet. Remove the dough from the bowl and gently knead a few times and form it into a smooth ball. Place on the parchment and let sit for about 2 more hours. It may or may not rise a bit.
- Place your Dutch oven in the oven and preheat to 450°F. When it's at temperature, pull it out and remove the lid (careful, it's hot!). Gently slash a few silts across the top of the dough with a knife or razor blade. Lift the dough by picking up the sides of the parchment. Carefully lower the loaf into the Dutch oven, then replace the lid, lower the oven temperature to 400°F, and bake for 45 minutes. After 45 minutes, take the lid off and bake for 15 more minutes.
- Let bread cool completely before slicing.

PART 6
THIS IS COMMITMENT

YOUR COMPLETE GUIDE TO SOURDOUGH

WAIT! ARE YOU A SCIENTIST?

No? Neither am I. But how many times have you heard that you need to be a scientist or good at math to bake bread? It's a common belief that anyone can cook, but that baking is this dark, mysterious world that uses exact measurements and temperatures and SCIENCE to create the beautiful breads. And the perfect loaf is only obtainable if you do the science.

Well guess what? I've won the California State Fair five years running with my sourdough bread, and I'm not a scientist. And I'm bad at math. And sometimes bad at following directions. I also didn't go to bread science school, I learned from a book and by baking a thousand loaves of bread. Some of those loaves came out flat like pancakes, some were burnt on the bottom and doughy in the middle, and some won the State Fair as the best sourdough bread in California. Go figure.

The key to learning how to make sourdough is to keep making sourdough! Find a reason to stay motivated. I look at it like this, making bread is a link to your past and part of your future. It's an ancient craft that we have forgotten how to do because life got in the way and someone else figured out how to make it cheaper and faster. But by taking this back from the world of mass food production, you now have the power to make a life-sustaining food right in your kitchen any time you want.

You can feed your family bread that has no added sugars, stabilizers, preservatives, or junk, AND it tastes amazing, and your house will smell like a bakery and love.

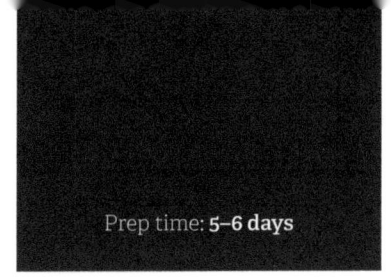

Prep time: **5–6 days**

SOURDOUGH STARTER

MAKE YOUR STARTER

plastic or glass bowl
about 1½ cups all-purpose flour
about 1½ cups whole wheat flour
about 1 cup water

To begin, you must start. That sounds very Yoda, but it's true. If you want to start making sourdough at home, the first thing you have to do is commit to the doing. It's a process and it takes time and patience, but you'll never get to the end if you don't start. So start it today!

- In order to make sourdough bread, you need the starter. You can buy starter or get some from a friend, but making your own is easy and kind of fun. You'll bond with your starter in the process, and it will quickly become a part of your family.

DAY 1

- In glass or plastic bowl, mix ¾ cup flour (white, wheat, or a mix, it doesn't matter) with ½ cup water. Cover with a towel and sit in a nice cozy spot in kitchen for 24 hours.

DAY 2

- Add in about a ¼ cup more flour, and a ¼ cup water to yesterday's mix. Stir and cover. Tomorrow, watch out for tiny bubbles. That's what we are after! The current bubbles you may see are from mixing, but fermenting bubbles will look very similar. Once we have bubbles, we are on the way!

DAY 3

- After day 3, you'll see lots of little bubbles. That's what we are looking for! This means yeast from the air has landed in the flour and water mix and are having a little non-social distancing party. Pour a bit out, then mix in about 2 tablespoons of flour and 2 tablespoons water and mix. Cover.

DAY 4 MORNING

- There should be clear or brownish liquid (hooch) forming on top. This is alcohol from the yeast eating the sugars in the flour. Pour off the hooch and then pour out about half of your starter. Refresh with 2 tablespoons flour and 2 tablespoons water, stir it up. By Day 4, it should start to have a scent other than flour paste. Slightly stinky, slightly sour, slightly fruity.

DAY 5

- You should see strong bubbles and it should have a pleasant but sour smell. It's now 100 percent ready-to-use sourdough starter made from scratch!

TIPS: You'll hear about using your discard in recipes, which means saving the starter when refreshing instead of pouring down the drain. Don't worry about that yet. When making the starter for the first time, it's best to just pour that bit down the drain.

- I make my starter in a plastic bowl, then once it gets going, I transfer it to a small Mason jar with a loose lid, no ring.
- If you are using it a lot, keep your starter out on the counter and covered with a loose lid. Every other day, pour out about a tablespoon of starter, then add back in a tablespoon of water and a tablespoon flour to keep it fed and happy.
- If you want to take a break from caring for your starter, put the ring on the Mason jar lid, then just put it all in the refrigerator. It'll sleep for months. To revive it, a few days before you want to bake, take it out, pour off any liquid, and scrape off any black gunk that may have formed. Then in a fresh jar, start feeding it again with a tablespoon of water and a tablespoon flour to wake it up again.
- If you have left it unattended too long, you'll get a gooey crust over the top. Sometimes it's just starter color, sometimes a little pinkish. Scrape that off, get a fresh jar, and add just a tablespoon of the starter that was under the goo, and then add a tablespoon of water and a tablespoon flour to revive it.
- If you have fuzzy mold, or greens and blues growing, or if it smells rotten, throw it all out. When in doubt, throw it out.
- Fruit flies love starter. Don't say you weren't warned.

AWARD-WINNING SOURDOUGH

Prep time: **45 minutes**
Proof time: **5 hours, then an overnight rest**
Bake time: **40 minutes**
Makes **2 loaves**

ADDITIONAL EQUIPMENT

You'll need two bamboo bannetons to rest the dough in if you want the cool-looking rings. You can use clean towels and bowls if you don't want to buy bannetons.

You'll also have the best success if you use a Dutch oven to bake the loaves in.

LEAVEN

½ cup all-purpose flour
½ cup whole wheat flour
1 cup water
1 tablespoon sourdough starter

DOUGH

3 cups water
1 cup active leaven
1½ cups whole wheat flour
5 cups all-purpose flour
1 tablespoon salt
½ cup water (additional)
Rice flour for dusting

This is a step-by-step guide to make my California State Fair award-winning sourdough bread. The recipe here makes two loaves. The most important part of the recipe is that you keep one loaf for yourself and family, and you give the other away. Sharing your bounty and newfound skills of bread baking will change your life.

DAY ONE, EVENING

- You now are the proud guardian of homemade sourdough starter, which you keep in a Mason jar on the counter and are regularly feeding at least once every two days. Before you go to bed, mix together a ½ cup of all-purpose flour and a ½ cup of whole wheat flour in a bowl, then with your finger or a spoon, stir in 1 tablespoon of your starter and a cup of water. Mix it all up, then cover with a towel and let it sit out overnight. This is called leaven now, not starter, but call it whatever you want.

- Then next morning, it should be a little puffy and may have bubbles on the surface. To see if it's ready to go, scoop out a teaspoon and put it in a cup of water. If it floats, you are ready to proceed. If not, let it sit longer until you can get a scoop to float.
- Floating? Let's go to Day 2.

DAY TWO, MORNING

- In a large bowl, pour in the 3 cups of warm water: warm but not hot. Pour 1 cup of the leaven you just made into the water and squish it all around, dissolving it into the water. The remaining leaven can now be used in a sourdough discard recipe, or it's your new starter. I usually just pour this back into the Mason jar with the little bit of remaining old starter. It makes your starter extra happy.
- Next, add in the 5 cups of all-purpose flour and the 1½ cups of whole wheat, and mix with your hand. It'll be a thick, lumpy dough. You'll need to squish hard with your hands to get all the flour incorporated into the water. Once

it's all mixed, cover with a towel and let sit for a half hour.

- After a half hour, sprinkle the 1 tablespoon of salt over the top, then pour the additional ¼ cup of water over the salt. Squish this all together with your hands until the water is all mixed in. Cover with the towel and let sit for another half hour.
- For the next 4–5 hours, every half hour you need to stretch and turn your dough. To do this, wet your fingers, and with one hand, reach down the inside of the bowl, grab some of the deep-down dough, and pull it up and over the top. Do this about 4 times per half hour, so that all the dough gets stretched and folded. You'll notice that after about an hour, the dough will start changing from wet flour to a smooth, stretchy, and pillowy dough.

- After 4–5 hours of stretching and folding, you are ready to start shaping. First, dust a cutting board with rice flour. Pour out the dough onto the board. With a dough scraper or knife, divide the dough in half by cutting down the middle. With your hands and the dough scraper, gently fold and move the two doughs into rough circle shapes. This isn't the final shape, so no need to be perfect. Cover with a towel and let sit on the board for 20 minutes. This is called the bench rest.
- While this is happening, prepare your bannetons or bowls. For the banneton, generously dust the insides with rice flour. Make sure you go all the way up and get into the cracks. You can also use a bowl with a clean, non-fuzzy kitchen towel. Drape the towel inside the bowl, then generously dust with rice flour.

- To shape the loaves, one at a time, sprinkle the tops with a little rice flour. Using the dough scraper, scoop the dough up and flip it over. The bottom will become the top of your loaf. You now need to do a series of pulls and folds. Pull on the bottom end of the dough, and fold up and over, then repeat on the sides and top until you have a round shape. Lift the round, and with the goal of getting surface tension on the lower side, let the dough sort of fall through your hands, squeezing toward the top. When you have a dough ball that's tight across the bottom, lower it into your banneton, tight side down. Don't worry how the top of the dough looks right now; it'll become the bottom tomorrow.
- Lay a towel over the bannetons, and place in the refrigerator and let it rest overnight. I find that 10–20 hours is the best. Under 10 hours doesn't give it enough time to develop flavors, and over 20 hours the dough starts losing its shape, and the dough can start drying out.

DAY THREE, MORNING

- I use Dutch ovens to bake my sourdough. For years, I only had one, so I'd bake loaf number one, then bake number two next. But eventually I bought a second, and now I do both loaves at once. You can bake on a baking sheet or a pizza stone, but you'll need to get some steam in the oven. The Dutch oven acts as a steamer as the bread bakes. If you are baking on a sheet, place a heavy-duty baking pan on the bottom rack of the oven, and add water right when you put the bread in (but be careful, don't splash water on the oven window or you may crack it!)
- Put your Dutch oven into the oven and heat it up to 500°F. From here on out, remember that the Dutch ovens, including the handle on the lid, are scorching hot! You'll only forget this once. Take your bannetons out of the fridge, and dust the top with rice flour, so it won't stick to the bottom of the Dutch oven. Remove the Dutch ovens and place them on top of the stove. Remove the lids. Over the sink so you don't make a mess, place your hand over the tops of the dough in the bannetons, and invert it so the dough drops into your palm. You may need to nudge it out but try to let gravity do the work here.

- Once in your hand, carefully lower it into the hot Dutch oven. Don't touch the sides! I use a razor blade to do my slashes, but you can be fancy and buy a bread lame. Either way, take your blade and make four quick, half-inch deep slashes across the top. I do a square pattern, but you can play around with this. The key is quick, mindful slashes with a sharp blade, so you are slashing rather than dragging the dough.
- Put lids back on (with oven mitt!) and put whole Dutch oven back in oven. Lower the temperature to 450°F and bake for 20 minutes. After 20 minutes, open oven and remove the lids (with oven mitts!) and bake for another 20 minutes.
- I like to put the empty bannetons on the top of the stove while the bread bakes because the heat from my oven dries them out. Once the bread comes out of the oven, I transfer the loaves from the Dutch ovens and sit them in the empty bannetons to let them cool. You can also just put them on a cooling rack. Let the loaves cool for a few hours before slicing into them as they are still cooking and firming up as they cool.

MIX IT UP

- Now that you have mastered my award-winning sourdough, it's time to mix it up. You can add all sorts of flavors and spices to your bread. Here are a few ideas, but the possibilities are endless. Just note, adding fresh, wet ingredients like blueberries or fresh figs can lead to your dough becoming a giant, wet mess. Stick to dried fruit when trying these out.

CINNAMON RAISIN SOURDOUGH

2 tablespoons cinnamon

1 tablespoon sugar

1 cup raisins

- Blend the cinnamon and sugar together. After you mix all the dough and start doing your stretch and folds, add in the cinnamon and sugar and raisins and continue to do the stretch and folds. The sugar will make the dough wetter than normal, but just keep going! It'll work.

LEMON, ROSEMARY, AND PINE NUT SOURDOUGH

2 tablespoons chopped rosemary

4 tablespoons pine nuts

zest from one lemon

2 teaspoons cracked pepper

- After you mix all the dough and start doing your stretch and folds, add in the new ingredients and continue to do the stretch and folds.

COCONUT, CHERRY, AND WALNUT SOURDOUGH

1 cup dried cherries
½ cup dried coconut flakes
1 cup chopped walnuts

- After you mix all the dough, and start doing your stretch and folds, add in the new ingredients and continue to do the stretch and folds.

CHEDDAR AND JALAPEÑO SOURDOUGH

1 cup cubed cheddar cheese (½-inch cubes)
½ cup pickled jalapeños, chopped

- After you mix all the dough and start doing your stretch and folds, add in the new ingredients and continue to do the stretch and folds.

Prep time: **30 minutes**
Proof time: **about 8 hours overnight, plus 1 hour the next day**
Bake time: **30 minutes**
Makes **about 12 four-inch muffins**

SOURDOUGH ENGLISH MUFFINS

½ cup sourdough starter (pancake batter consistency)
1 cup milk
2¾ cups all-purpose flour
1 tablespoon sugar
1 teaspoon baking soda
1 teaspoon salt
cornmeal for dusting

English muffins are fairly easy to make. This recipe requires an overnight rest, so start these the night before. The good thing is they come together pretty quickly the next morning. Just a mix, roll out and cut out, then an hour proof. They cook in a pan for just a few minutes, so you don't need to worry about heating up the whole house. You can freeze any extra muffins and use them as needed for your butter and jelly delivery needs.

MAKE THE LEAVEN (DO THIS THE NIGHT BEFORE)

- First, you'll need a half cup of sourdough starter. If you have a half cup to spare from the jar you keep, just use that. If you don't, mix ¼ flour with ¼ cup water, then add a tablespoon of your starter and mix again, then use that.
- Mix the ½ cup starter, 2 cups of flour, and the 1 cup milk in a bowl, and cover. Let it sit out overnight. It's fine. The milk is fine. Don't worry.

MAKE THE MUFFINS

- The next morning, add the additional ¾ cup flour, salt, and baking soda to the mix. Stir to incorporate, then pour out onto a flour dusted cutting board and knead for a few minutes until the dough is soft and smooth. On same cutting board, roll out the dough to be about a ½ inch thick and let rest for a few minutes. While waiting, take a parchment-lined baking sheet and sprinkle with cornmeal. Now, using a round cutter—an empty tin can will work too—cut out as many muffins as you can. Transfer them to the cornmeal baking sheet. If you have scraps, you can roll them back up into a ball, roll it out, and cut a few more.
- Cover and let rise for at least an hour.
- Heat a cast-iron skillet or heavy pan to medium on the stovetop. Add a little oil. A few at a time, gently place the muffins in the pan. Cook the muffins for about 3 minutes, then flip and cook for about 3 to 4 more minutes. They will be golden brown on the top and bottom.
- Remember, always split your muffins with a fork for maximum nook, maximum cranny.

Prep time: 15 minutes
Proof time: about 30 minutes
Bake time: 22 minutes
Makes 8 large crackers

SOURDOUGH CRACKERS

NOTE

Make 8 large crackers, which you can break into whatever size smaller crackers you want

INGREDIENTS

1 cup sourdough starter, can be the extra from making your loaves
½ cup all-purpose flour
½ cup whole wheat flour
3 tablespoons extra virgin olive oil
1 tablespoon Everything Bagel seasoning
½ teaspoon fine sea salt
Maldon flake salt

Crackers are a great way to use up extra sourdough starter you might have. If you don't have a cup to spare, just mix equal parts flour with water and add a little starter, let it sit for a few hours, and you'll have extra! You can add just about anything to these crackers to change them up...dried herbs, parmesan cheese, hot peppers...

- In a bowl, mix everything together except the Maldon flake salt, that'll be for sprinkling on top. Mix together and form into a ball, cover and let sit in the refrigerator for about a half an hour and up to a few days.
- Preheat oven to 350°F. Take the dough out and divide the dough into eight pieces. Lightly flour a cutting board and roll out each piece as thin as you can. Like, super thin. Lay them on a parchment-lined baking sheet.
- Lightly brush them with water, and sprinkle with the Maldon flake salt.
- Bake for about 22 minutes, watching carefully so they don't burn, maybe even rotating the baking sheets halfway through. When lightly brown and crispy, remove from oven. Let cool, then break apart the crackers into desired size.

PART 7
BREAD IDEAS

RECIPES USING SOME OF THE BREADS IN THIS BOOK

BREAD IDEAS

Bread and butter. Bread and jam. Toast. Really, what else do you need? Most of the recipes in this book are stand alone, delicious breads. But sometimes, you want to take your bread to the next level. Sometimes you have extra bread that you don't know what to do with.

The following pages include my favorite recipes for extra or leftover bread. For most of these recipes, you can use any of the breads in this book. Obviously, you won't use the cinnamon rolls or the blueberry babka for breadcrumbs or burger buns, but I trust your judgement.

BREADCRUMBS & CROUTONS

If you ever happen to have leftover bread, don't let it go to waste. Breadcrumbs and croutons (which is a great jug band name, by the way) are a perfect way to keep the bread going. Day-old bread is best for these. You can even keep a Ziploc bag in the freezer and toss in any leftover heels and odds and ends, then defrost to make a bigger batch of these. Any of the regular loaves will work here, from sourdough to challah.

BREADCRUMBS

day-old bread, cut or torn into cubes
salt

Homemade breadcrumbs are great to have on hand. You can use them as toppings for casseroles, breading on chicken and fish, and to add to meatballs or meatloaf.

- Let the cubed bread sit out for a day or so, so it's very dry and starts to harden. Place in food processor or blender and grind up into coarse crumbs. Preheat your oven to 300°F. Spread the crumbs on a baking sheet, sprinkle with a bit of salt, then bake for about 15 minutes, stirring the crumbs every 5 minutes. Remove and let cool.
- When cool, put in an airtight Ziploc or Mason jar to store. Will keep for months.

CROUTONS

Bump up your soup and salad game with homemade croutons. They are easy to make, and you get bonus points for using bread that may normally go to waste.

4 or so cups of day-old bread, cut or torn into cubes

¼ cup olive oil, butter, or bacon fat

1 teaspoon garlic powder

1 teaspoon onion powder

1 teaspoon black pepper

1 teaspoon salt

- Preheat oven to 375°F. In a large bowl, toss all the ingredients to coat the bread in oil and spices. Spread out in an even layer on a parchment-lined baking sheet. Bake until golden brown, turning them every once in a while to keep them from burning, about 15 minutes.

NOTE: You can also make these in a pan on the stovetop, making a smaller batch that can fit in a pan.

- When cool, put in an airtight Ziploc. They'll keep for about a week.

Prep time: **25 minutes**
Serves **about 4**

FRIED GREEN TOMATOES WITH PICKLED CORN & PEPPERS

3 large green tomatoes
¾ cup breadcrumbs
½ cup milk
1 egg
1 cup all-purpose flour
1 teaspoon smoked paprika
salt

Here is an excellent use of the homemade breadcrumbs you just made. Find hard, solid green tomatoes with no ripe parts for this. Serve this as a summer appetizer or go all out and make this a hearty vegetarian sandwich by placing a few of these fried green tomatoes between two slices of bread, add the remoulade and corn, then add some lettuce and maybe a round slice of fresh mozzarella.

- Slice the tomatoes into quarter-inch thick slices, salt them, and set aside. Make a line-up of three bowls on your counter:
    1. flour and the smoked paprika
    2. the milk and egg beaten together
    3. the breadcrumbs.
- Heat a skillet with olive oil to medium. Take a tomato, coat it in the flour, then dip into the milk/egg mixture, then dredge it in the breadcrumbs. Fry them in the pan a few at a time for about 3-4 minutes per side. Salt and pepper when done.
- To make the plate, stack a few fried green tomatoes, then add a bloop of remoulade, then spoon some of the pickled corn mix over the top.

SWEET PICKLE RÉMOULADE

¼ cup Dijon mustard
1 cup mayo
2 teaspoons pickle juice
1 gherkin pickle, finely chopped
1 teaspoon hot sauce
1 garlic clove, chopped
1 tablespoon smoked paprika
2 teaspoons Cajun seasoning
1 tablespoon chopped parsley

- Combine all ingredients, then refrigerate for a few hours to meld together.

QUICK PICKLED CORN & CHILI PEPPER RELISH

5–6 seeded hot peppers, whatever kind you want
¼ cup thinly sliced onion
2 cups fresh corn kernels
¼ teaspoon black pepper
½ cup apple cider vinegar
¾ cup water
2 teaspoons salt
1 teaspoon sugar

- Mix the corn, peppers, black pepper, and onion in a bowl, then pack into a quart-sized Mason jar, leaving about a half-inch at the top.
- In a pot on the stove, bring the vinegar, water, sugar, and salt to a boil. Pour the boiling water into the jar, covering the corn mix. If you need more liquid, just top with a little more vinegar. Put the lid on and seal, then let cool. When cool, move to refrigerator until ready to use.

FRIED GREEN TOMATOES WITH PICKLED CORN & PEPPERS

Prep time: **15 minutes**
Makes about **4 servings**

WATERMELON, TOMATO PANZANELLA

The addition of cold watermelon brings a welcome sweetness to the acidic tomatoes. Make sure you grab a wide selection of colors, shapes, and sizes of tomatoes to create a knock-out presentation. Add chicken or bacon to turn this salad into dinner.

- In a large bowl, gently toss all the ingredients with the vinaigrette, then place in individual serving bowls.

NOTE

The quantities listed here are a suggestion. If you like more watermelon, more tomatoes, or more croutons, just add more.

INGREDIENTS

2 large heirloom tomatoes, or a mix and match of different colors and sizes
2 cups cold, cubed watermelon pieces
2 cups homemade croutons
5–6 bocconcini-size fresh mozzarella balls
fresh torn basil
salt and pepper
heirloom tomato vinaigrette

HEIRLOOM TOMATO VINAIGRETTE

1 large, very ripe tomato
¼ cup olive oil
1 tablespoon Dijon mustard
1 tablespoon honey
1 teaspoon salt

- Toss all in a blender and blend until smooth. Adjust taste with salt or honey if needed.

BREADS, SPREADS & TOASTS

Prep time: **10 minutes**
Makes **2 sandwiches**

GRILLED SOFT PRETZEL WITH TURKEY AND CHEESE

2 fresh-baked soft pretzels (recipe page 37)
4 slices of provolone cheese
sliced turkey
sauerkraut
mayo
honey mustard
butter for toasting

I figure you already know you can make a killer grilled cheese with the breads in this book. This is a slightly different grilled cheese you may have not thought of.

- Slice the pretzels in half. Add a layer of mayo, then one slice of provolone cheese, then turkey, sauerkraut, then top with the second piece of cheese, finally adding the top part of the pretzel. Heat a pan on the stove and melt about a tablespoon of butter in the pan. Add the sandwich and gently grill it like you would a grilled cheese sandwich, flipping it halfway through, until the cheese has melted.
- Place the sandwich on your plate, take the top off, drizzle with Honey Mustard (see page 155), and enjoy!

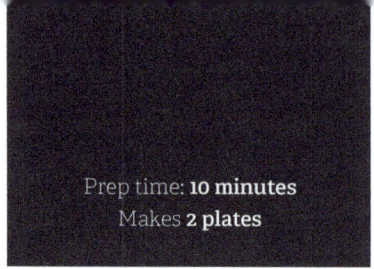

Prep time: **10 minutes**
Makes **2 plates**

OPEN-FACE TOMATO SANDWICH

4 slices of bread, green onion Pullman here (recipe page 57), but most breads in this book would work
fresh goat cheese, softened
fresh basil
2 heirloom tomatoes, sliced thick
salt and pepper, to taste

Sometimes, simplicity is the best way to go. Whenever I see a giant, misshapen tomato, I remember the tomatoes my grandpa used to grow in his garden. My dad used to just slice them up and eat them with mayo and salt and pepper. This is that, on a plate.

- This isn't so much a recipe as it is an assembly. Toast the bread, spread with goat cheese (or mayo!), lay down a few basil leaves, top with the tomato slices. Salt and pepper to taste and enjoy.

TIP: If available, use a few different varieties of heirloom tomatoes for a beautiful presentation.

OPEN-FACE TOMATO SANDWICH

Prep time: **10 minutes**
Makes **2 plates**

AVOCADO TOAST

4 slices of bread (most breads in this book would work)
1 ripe avocado
a few strips of roasted peppers, fresh or jarred
8 cherry tomatoes, halved
fresh cilantro
squirt of lime juice
dusting of cotija cheese
salt and pepper to taste

Be hip. Avocado toast. All day. Everyday.

- Toast the bread, spread with mashed up avocado, then add peppers, top with the tomato halves and cilantro. Sprinkle the whole thing with cotija cheese. Salt and pepper and a squirt of lime to taste and enjoy.

TIP: Add a fried sunny-side-up egg to this to make a hearty breakfast.

FOCACCIA BLT

2 big squares of Lemon, Rosemary Tomato, Focaccia (recipe page 81)
6 strips cooked, crispy bacon
4 thick slices of heirloom tomato
2 lettuce leaves
mayo
salt and pepper

Simple sandwiches depend on the best ingredients. Crisp bacon. Cold lettuce. Juicy heirloom tomatoes. Creamy mayonnaise. Fresh-baked bread. I'm using the Lemon, Rosemary, Tomato Focaccia here, but sourdough, whole wheat, and any of the white loaves would be a perfect stand-in.

- Slice the squares of focaccia in half to make a sandwich. Starting with the mayo, all the lettuce, then tomato, then bacon. Salt and pepper to taste.

Prep time: **15 minutes**
Makes **2 plates**

CORN, CHILES AND TOMATO TOASTS

2 ears of corn, husked
4 Hatch chiles (or canned roasted Hatch chiles)
1 tablespoon olive oil
handful of cherry tomatoes, sliced in half
torn fresh basil
goat cheese
4 slices of No-Knead Artisan Jalapeño Cheddar Loaf (recipe page 54)
salt and pepper

This toast can be breakfast, lunch, dinner, and anything in between. Beware of falling corns.

- In a pan, heat the olive. Cut the corn off the ears and add them to the pan. Chop and seed the chiles (or open can if using that) and add to the corn with a little salt. Sautee for about 10 minutes until the corn starts to caramelize and turn brown and the chiles are cooked through (they'll turn from bright green to more of an olive green).
- Slice a few pieces of bread and toast them. To assemble, spread a layer of goat cheese, then add the corn chile mix, then top with fresh basil and fresh cherry tomatoes. Salt and pepper to taste.

CORN, CHILES AND TOMATO TOASTS

Prep time: 5 minutes
Makes 1 cup

LEMON RICOTTA SPREAD

1 cup fresh ricotta cheese
1 tablespoon sugar
zest of one lemon
1 teaspoon chopped thyme or rosemary

This spread couldn't be easier to make or more delicious with a hunk of fresh sourdough.

- Mix all the ingredients. Save a tiny bit of zest and rosemary to sprinkle over the top to look pretty.

Prep time: **10 minutes**
Makes **about a cup**

JAPANESE EGGPLANT SPREAD

1–2 long Japanese eggplants, sliced (about 2 cups worth)
1 clove garlic
1 tablespoon minced ginger
2 tablespoons olive oil
2 tablespoons rice wine vinegar
1 tablespoon soy sauce
1 tablespoon sugar
1 teaspoon cornstarch
sesame seeds for garnish

This becomes a perfect spread to dip toasted Furikake Pita Chips (recipe page 33) into. You can also try adding some fresh corn and zucchini while you make it, and it'll become a delicious side dish for a chicken or fish dinner.

- In a pan, heat the oil on medium and add in the garlic and ginger. Cook for just a minute, then add in the eggplant. Sautee for a few minutes until the oil is pretty much soaked up by the eggplants.
- Meanwhile, in a small bowl, mix together the vinegar, soy sauce, sugar, and corn starch.
- Reduce the heat and pour in the soy sauce mixture. Cook for about 10 more minutes until the eggplants are super tender and starting to fall apart.
- Move to a serving bowl, and sprinkle with sesame seeds to serve.

JAPANESE EGGPLANT SPREAD

BURGERTIME

THE SUMMER CLASSIC BURGER

Prep time: **25 minutes to cook and assemble**
Makes **4 burgers**

This is my favorite summer burger. It has my three favorite summer ingredients: fresh local corn, plump heirloom tomatoes, and grassy basil. Gather your produce at the farmers market in the morning, come home and start your fresh-baked buns, then light up the grill and go for it.

TO MAKE THIS BURGER

- 1 pound grass-fed ground beef
- mayo
- 4 slices provolone cheese
- Corn & Chile Peppers (see below)
- fresh basil
- fresh tomato
- sunflower sprouts
- salt & pepper
- 4 Fresh-Baked Burger Buns (recipe page 30)

TO MAKE THE BURGER

- Divide the beef into 4 equal patties, and generously salt and pepper. In pan or on a grill, cook burgers for about 4–5 minutes, then flip for another 2–3 minutes. Add a slice of cheese and melt.
- Cut your buns, then butter and toast them.
- Start with the bottom bun, add a smear of mayo, add the sunflower sprouts, then top that with the burger with the cheese, add tomato, then a scoop of the Corn & Chile Peppers and a few basil leaves and sprouts, finally topping with the top bun.

CORN & CHILE PEPPERS

- 2 ears of corn, husked
- 4 Hatch chiles (or canned roasted Hatch chiles)
- 1 tablespoon olive oil
- salt and pepper

- In a pan, heat the olive. Cut the corn off the ears and add them to the pan. Chop and seed the chiles (or open can) and add to corn with a little salt. Sautee for about 10 minutes until the corn starts to brown and the chiles are cooked through (they'll turn from bright green to more of an olive green).

Prep time: 25 minutes
Serves about 4

TINY POTATO PARTY

1 pound of the tiniest potatoes you can find
1–2 cloves garlic, thinly sliced
1 tablespoon olive oil
1 tablespoon butter
a sprinkle of fresh rosemary or thyme
lots of salt and pepper

There's a guy at my farmers market who sells potatoes in their tiniest form, almost the size of little marbles. You can also find them in specialty grocery stores. If you are grilling, put a cast-iron pan right on the grill and make these while you are doing the burgers. You can also do them on the stovetop. You'll never want a French fry again.

- Heat up a cast-iron or heavy-duty pan. Add the oil and butter and toss in the potatoes. They should take about 20–30 minutes to fully cook, depending on their size. After about 10 minutes, add the garlic (so it won't burn) and salt and pepper throughout the cooking time. Finish by tossing in the fresh herbs.
- Any leftovers can be added to your eggs in the morning!

BREAD PUDDINGS

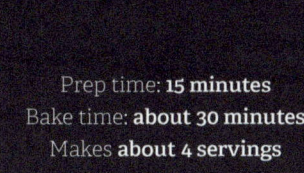

Prep time: **15 minutes**
Bake time: **about 30 minutes**
Makes **about 4 servings**

SAVORY BREAD PUDDING

- 2–3 cups stale bread, torn into small pieces
- 1 cup cheese (I used cheddar)
- 1 cup veggies (I used corn and purple cabbage)
- ½ cup chopped meat, if you want (I used salami)
- 1 tablespoon fresh herbs (I used thyme)
- 2 eggs
- ½ cup milk
- ½ cup heavy cream or half and half
- 1 tablespoon mustard
- 1 teaspoon salt
- 1 teaspoon pepper

Have leftover bread? Leftover veggies? A little leftover meat from last night? Excellent! Toss whatever you have together, soak it with a little custard mixture, and bake. The possibilities here are endless!

- In an oven proof baking dish or cast-iron pan, oil or butter the sides and bottom. Spread the bread in a layer on the bottom, then add in the veggies, cheese, meat, and herbs. In a small bowl, whisk the eggs, cream, milk, and mustard together, and pour over everything. Add salt and pepper. Let it all sit for a while until the bread soaks up the egg milk mixture, about 15 minutes.
- Preheat oven to 375°F. Bake in oven for about 45–50 minutes. It's done when it's cooked through in the center and golden brown on top.

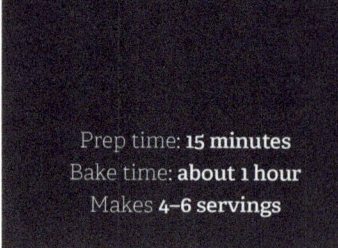

Prep time: **15 minutes**
Bake time: **about 1 hour**
Makes **4–6 servings**

BERRY BREAD PUDDING

- 4 cups day-old bread, torn into small pieces
- 2 cups mixed berries, cut into pieces (strawberries, blueberries, raspberries)
- 1 cup sugar
- 4 eggs
- 1 cup milk
- ½ cup heavy cream or half and half
- 1 teaspoon vanilla extract
- 1 teaspoon salt
- whipped cream or ice cream for serving

This sweet berry bread pudding can cover you in many situations. Breakfast? Brunch? Dessert? Mid-day snack? It's got you! Most of the breads will work here, but sourdough and the white breads are best. You can also try many different fruits to mix things up. Just replace the berries with equal parts other fruit.

- In an oven proof baking dish or cast-iron pan, oil or butter the sides and bottom. Spread the bread in a layer on the bottom, then add in the berries. In a small bowl, whisk the eggs, sugar, vanilla, salt, milk, and cream together, and pour over everything. Let it all sit for a while until the bread soaks up the egg milk mixture, about 15 minutes. You can also cover and put in the fridge and let sit up to 24 hours.
- Preheat oven to 375°F. Bake in oven for about 45–50 minutes. It's done when it's cooked through in the center and golden brown on top. Cut into squares and serve with whipped cream or ice cream.

CONCHA BREAD PUDDING

Prep time: **15 minutes**
Bake time: **about 45 minutes**
Makes **6–8 servings**

4–5 conchas, can be day old, cubed (recipe page 78)
1½ cups milk
½ cup cream or half and half
3 eggs
1 cup sugar
1 tablespoon ground cinnamon
2 teaspoons almond extract
2 tablespoons slivered almonds
powdered sugar, for dusting

You will probably only have leftover conchas if you have turned your kitchen into a recipe test kitchen and have made eight different batches trying to get the recipe right. If you do happen to have extra, this will knock your socks off.

- Grease an eight-by-eight-inch baking dish (or similar size) with butter or oil. Add in the cubed conchas, making sure you leave a few with the sugary tops facing up, so it'll look better when baked. In a bowl, whisk together the milk, eggs, sugar, cinnamon, and almond extract. Pour the egg mix over the conchas, so almost all the bread gets wet. Sprinkle the almond slivers over the top. Let sit for about 15 minutes.
- Preheat the oven to 350°F. Bake for about 40–45 minutes. Let cool, then slice into squares and top with powdered sugar.

Bake time: **about 8 minutes**
Makes **as many twelve-inch pizzas you have doughs for**

PIZZA, PIZZA!

SPECIAL EQUIPMENT

Wooden pizza peel (this will be so helpful, but you can also use an upside-down baking tray, but it's a little more difficult to control)

Pizza stone (again, this will help with a perfect pizza bake, but you can also use a baking sheet)

INGREDIENTS

ready to go pizza doughs (recipe page 61)
½ cup of rice flour, in a bowl
pizza toppings of your choice

- Preheat your oven with the pizza stone in it to 500°F.
- Generously dust your pizza peel with rice flour. Take one dough, place it in the rice flour bowl, and coat it all over. Gently start pressing down to make a disk rather than ball. Now move the dough to a cutting board, and with your fingers, start pushing down and out, gently stretching the dough on all sides, making about a ten-inch disk. Pick it up, and with your hands, hold the edges and let gravity pull and stretch the dough even thinner until you have about a fourteen-inch round dough. Place the dough on the peel (it'll shrink back a bit; try to keep it about twelve inches across).
- Now add your toppings. Sauce, cheese, veggies, and meats, and more cheese. Sprinkle with salt. Slide into the oven onto the pizza stone and bake for about 8 minutes until the cheese and the crust starts to brown.
- Use the peel to now remove it. Let cool for a moment, then cut into pieces and nom nom nom. Repeat.

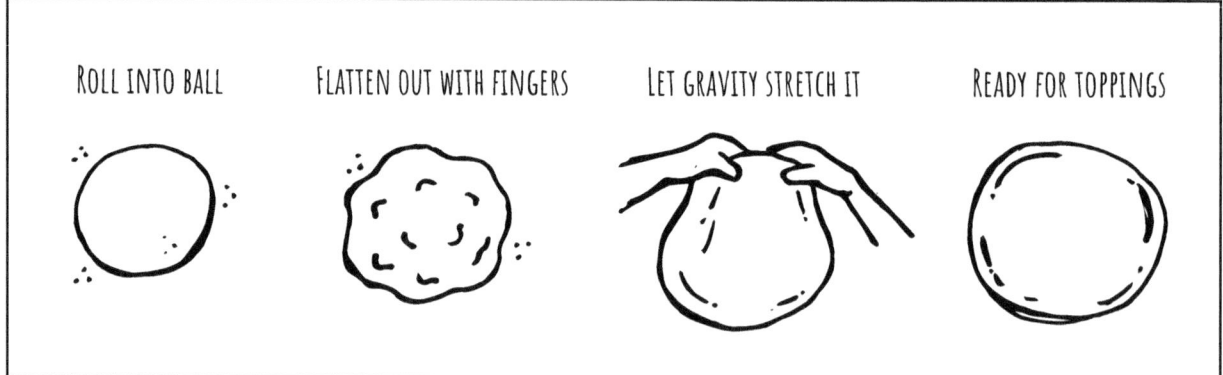

BREAD BAKING BASICS

SALAMI, PINEAPPLE, AND CORN PIZZA

pizza sauce
mozzarella cheese
fresh pineapple
thin cut salami
fresh corn kernels

- Start with your favorite pizza sauce, add cheese, and then salami, corn, and pineapple, then top with more cheese. Bake.

PEAR, BRIE, AND ONIONS

caramelized onions
mozzarella cheese
fresh pears, sliced
brie
pine nuts
fresh thyme

- Another no-sauce pizza! Start with a layer of mozzarella, then add onions, pears, strips of brie, pine nuts, and thyme. Bake.

BBQ, PICKLED CORN AND PEPPERS, SAUSAGE

BBQ sauce
Quick Pickled Corn & Chili Pepper Relish (recipe page 125)
cooked spicy sausage
mozzarella cheese

- Use your favorite BBQ sauce, the add a little cheese, the sausage and relish, then more cheese. Bake.

POTATO, BACON AND BLUE

caramelized onions
boiled small Yukon Gold potatoes, cooled and thinly sliced
crumbled bacon
mozzarella cheese
blue cheese
pine nuts
fresh thyme

- This is also a no-sauce pizza. Start with a layer of mozzarella, then add onions, potatoes, bacon, pine nuts, and thyme. Crumble blue cheese over the top. Bake.

FIG, GOAT CHEESE, AND BACON

caramelized onions
fresh figs, sliced
crumbled bacon
mozzarella cheese
goat cheese
pine nuts

- This is a no-sauce pizza. Add a little mozzarella cheese, then the figs, bacon, pine nuts, and onions. Top with goat cheese and bake.

Prep time: **20 minutes**

PRETZEL TRAY DIPPERS

Make a charcuterie board with soft pretzels instead of crackers. Add some salami, cheese, fruits and veggies, and a trio of dipping sauces!

HONEY MUSTARD

¼ cup honey
¼ cup mayonnaise
¼ cup Dijon mustard
1 tablespoon white distilled vinegar
cracked pepper

- Whisk everything together until smooth.

JALAPEÑO IPA CHEESE

¼ cup butter
2 tablespoons all-purpose flour
1 teaspoon garlic powder
1 cup milk
half-can of IPA beer
2 teaspoons Dijon mustard
2 cups cheddar, shredded
3 tablespoons pickled jalapeños, chopped

- In a pot on the stove, melt the butter, then whisk in the flour and garlic powder, and cook for a few minutes. Pour in the milk, beer, and mustard, and mix until warm. Slowly add in the cheese until smooth and melty, then stir in the jalapeños.

RANCH!

½ cup mayonnaise
¼ cup Greek yogurt
¾ cup buttermilk
2 teaspoons chives
1 teaspoon dill
1 teaspoon parsley
1 teaspoon onion powder
½ teaspoon salt
½ teaspoon pepper

- Mix all ingredients together until blended.

BREADY DESSERTS

Prep time: **10 minutes**
Makes **2 plates**

SEÑORITA BREAD WAFFLES

4-day-old (or fresh) Señiorita Bread
(recipe page 46)
fresh strawberries and blueberries
butter for waffle iron
powdered sugar for dusting

This is a great dessert to serve, as well as just a nice Sunday breakfast. It's a good way to use day-old pastries that may have gotten a bit stale. Throw them in the waffle maker! Top with fresh fruit! Be fancy and give it a shake of powdered sugar!

- Again, this is super simple, but that's because you already put in the effort to make the Señorita Breads in the first place. Pop them in a buttered waffle iron, and toast until the waffle maker beeps. Serve with fresh fruit (add whipped cream if you are feeling extra) and top with a sprinkle of powdered sugar.

TIP: For the best powdered sugar dusting, put a bit of powdered sugar into a mesh strainer, then over the plate, gently bop the side of the strainer, and it'll make a little powdered sugar snowfall.

STRAWBERRY SHORTCAKES

Prep time: **10 minutes**
Makes **4 plates**

1 cup heavy whipping cream, cold
2 tablespoons sugar
½ teaspoon vanilla extract
4 fresh-baked biscuits
2 cups chopped fresh strawberries and blueberries, mixed

There's something to be said about those premade Twinkie-like shortcakes from the store, but have you tried strawberry shortcake with homemade everything? You'll never buy those things again. Try adding other fresh fruit like watermelon cubes, sliced nectarines, or plums to the mix, too.

- In the bowl of a standing mixer (I actually have a hand-held immersion blender that works great), whip together the cold whipping cream, sugar, and vanilla. Whip for 3–4 minutes until stiff peaks form when you pull out the whisk.
- Slice open a warm biscuit, then layer whipped cream and fruit, then top with the biscuit top.

TIP: Make sure the whipping cream is cold or it won't hold its shape. If it does start losing its shape, just whip it again.

STRAWBERRY SHORTCAKES

ACKNOWLEDGEMENTS

You can't write a bread baking book without acknowledging the fact that these recipes were developed over centuries and across continents and cultures. I've taken tried and true recipes, tweaked and updated them, and added something and subtracted something in order to streamline the ingredients and steps to help you be a more successful home baker. All bakers are standing on the shoulders of the croissants and conchas that came before us.

I couldn't do this, the baking and writing and photographing and illustrating, without the loving support of my wife, Lori, and the more than-honest-feedback from my ten-year-old, Rowan, who will straight up tell me when someone else's bread is better than mine.

ABOUT THE AUTHOR

Gregory Berger was a full-time, stay-at-home dad running his own successful company when he was first inspired to make bread. Between diaper changes and the graphic design work he does for restaurants and nonprofits through his company, Pomegranate Design, Greg read a book about sourdough bread. He baked one loaf and it sparked a passion. He has earned a slew of blue ribbons at the California State Fair for his breads. He now creates original bread recipes for some of the top restaurants in Northern California. Greg is also well known for baking buns and rolls for charity events that draw thousands, including the Sacramento Burger Battle and the Sacramento Sausage Fest.

His first book, *Buns & Burgers: Handcrafted Burgers from Top to Bottom*, inspired home bakers worldwide to learn how to make their own buns. You can find recipes, tips, and inspiration by following his blog, The Fresh Bread Daily.

WWW.THEFRESHBREADDAILY.COM

INSTAGRAM:
THEFRESHBREADDAILY

FACEBOOK:
THEFRESHBREADDAILY

YOUTUBE:
THEFRESHBREADDAILY

MY FAVORITE BREAD RESOURCES

BOOKS

Tartine Bread by Chad Robertson

The Sullivan Street Bakery Cookbook by Jim Lahey

Bravetart by Stella Parks

Black Girl Baking by Jerrelle Guy

Bread Baking for Beginners by Bonnie Ohara

WEBSITE

Sally's Baking Addiction—www.sallysbakingaddiction.com

MY FAVORITE PRODUCTS

For flour, Central Milling—www.centralmilling.com

I use Red Start Yeast—www.redstaryeast.com

If you want to buy a starter, try Ed Wood's Sourdough International—www.sourdo.com

I find most of my tools and equipment on Amazon.com or kingarthurbaking.com

INDEX

A

Active dry yeast: 9, 17, 26, 29-30, 33, 37, 42, 45-46, 54, 57, 61-62, 65-66, 69, 77-78, 81-82, 90, 93-94

All-purpose flour: 17, 26, 29-30, 33-34, 37-38, 41-42, 45-46, 49-50, 54, 57, 61-62, 65-66, 69, 77-78, 81-82, 101, 105, 114, 117, 124, 155

Almond
    Blueberry Almond Muffins with Crumbly Top: 38
    Chocolate Cherry Almond Scones: 41
    Concha Bread Pudding: 149

Apple cider vinegar: 125

Artisan loaf
    Gluten-Free Artisan Loaf: 94
    No-knead Artisan Cheddar Jalapeño Bread: 54, 134

B

Babka
    Blueberry Cream Cheese Babka: 66

Bacon: 127, 133, 153-154

Bagels
    Candied Orange Pretzeled Bagels: 82

Baking powder: 34, 38, 41, 50, 78, 94

Baking soda: 34, 37-38, 49, 82, 114

Biscuits
    Big, Fat Biscuits: 34, 160

Blueberries: 38, 65-66, 108, 146, 159-160

Bread pudding
    Berry Bread Pudding: 146
    Concha Bread Pudding: 149
    Savory Bread Pudding: 145

Breadcrumbs: 46, 120, 122, 124

Burger bun
    The Easiest Burger Bun: 30, 141

Butter: 18, 26, 29-30, 34, 37-38, 41-42, 45-46, 49-50, 57-58, 65-66, 69, 77-78, 90, 114, 120, 123, 129, 141-142, 145-146, 149, 155, 159

Buttermilk: 34, 77, 155

C

Challah: 62, 120

Charcuterie: 155

Cheese: 37, 41, 49, 54, 66, 75, 77, 82, 113, 117, 129-130, 132, 134, 137, 141, 145, 150-155

Cherry: 38, 41, 112

Chocolate: 38, 41, 66, 69, 74

Cinnamon: 38, 46, 65-66, 77-78, 110, 149

Cinnamon rolls
    Buttermilk Cinnamon Rolls with Cinnamon Icing: 77

Concha Bread Pudding: 149

Corn: 124-125, 134, 138, 141, 145, 151-152

Crackers
    Sourdough Crackers: 117

Cream cheese: 49, 66, 77, 82

Croissants
    Croissants Two Ways: 69-71
    Ham and Swiss Croissants with Thyme: 75
    Pain au Chocolat: 74

Croutons: 33, 120, 123, 127

D

Dips
    Honey Mustard: 37, 129, 155
    Jalapeño IPA Cheese: 37, 155
    Ranch!: 155

Donuts
    Blueberry Donuts: 65

Desserts
    Berry Bread Pudding: 146
    Blueberry Donuts: 65
    Concha Bread Pudding: 149
    Señorita Bread Waffles: 159
    Strawberry Shortcakes: 160

Dutch ovens: 54, 94, 105, 107-108

E

English muffins: 114

Everything bagel seasoning: 82, 117

Equipment: 14-15, 105, 150, 164

F

Flatbread
    Quick and Easy Flatbreads: 50

Flour: 9-10, 13, 17-18, 26, 29-30, 33-34, 37-38, 41-42, 45-46, 49-50, 54, 57, 61-62, 65-66, 69, 77-78, 81-82, 88, 90, 93-94, 101, 103, 105-107, 114, 117, 124, 150, 155, 164
Figs: 108, 154
Focaccia
    Gluten-Free Focaccia: 90
    Lemon, Rosemary, Tomato Focaccia: 81, 133
Fried Green Tomatoes with Pickled Corn
    & Peppers: 124
Furikake: 33, 138

G

Gluten Free
    About: 17, 88
    Artisan Loaf: 94
    Focaccia: 90
    Pizza Crust: 93
Green Onions: 57, 130

I

Icing: 65, 77

J

Jalapeños
    Cheddar and Jalapeño Sourdough: 113
    Jalapeño IPA Cheese: 37, 155
    No-Knead Artisan Cheddar Jalapeño Bread: 54, 134

L

Lemon
    Focaccia BLT: 133
    Lemon, Rosemary, and Pine Nut Sourdough: 111
    Lemon, Rosemary, Tomato Focaccia: 81
    Lemon Ricotta Spread: 137

M

Milk bread
    Japanese Milk Bread: 42, 45
Milk rolls
    Hokkaido Milk Rolls: 45
Muffins
    Blueberry Almond Muffins with Crumbly Top: 38
    Sourdough English Muffins: 114

N

No-knead bread: 54, 134
Nuts: 38, 41, 49, 111, 112, 149, 152-154

O

Onions: 14, 125, 152-154
Oranges
    Candied Orange Peels: 83
    Candied Orange Pretzeled Bagels: 82

P

Panzanella: 127
Peppers: 117, 124-125, 132, 141, 152
Pickles
    Quick Pickled Corn & Chili Pepper Relish: 125, 152
    Sweet Pickle Rémoulade: 124
Pine nuts: 111, 152-154
Pita
    Furikake Pita Bread: 33
    Japanese Eggplant Spread: 138
Pizza
    BBQ, Pickled Corn and Peppers, Sausage: 152
    Fig, Goat Cheese, and Bacon: 154
    Pear, Brie, and Onion: 152
    Potato, Bacon, and Blue: 153
    Salami, Pineapple, and Corn: 151
Pizza crust
    Perfect Pizza Crust: 61
    Gluten-Free Pizza Dough: 93
Potato: 88, 142, 153
Powdered sugar: 65, 77, 149, 159
Proofing: 15, 18, 22, 26, 29-30, 33, 37, 41-42, 45-46, 49-50, 54, 57, 61-62, 65-66, 77-78, 81-82, 90, 93-94, 105, 114, 117
Pullman bread
    Green Onion Pullman Bread: 57
    Open-Face Tomato Sandwich: 130
Pretzels
    Candied Orange Pretzeled Bagels: 82
    Grilled Soft Pretzel with Turkey and Cheese: 129
    Pretzel Tray Dippers: 155
    Soft Pretzels & Pretzel Bites: 37
Pretzel Tray Dippers: 155

Q

Quick Breads
    Chocolate Cherry Almond Scones: 41
    Biscuits: 34, 160
    Blueberry Almond Muffins with Crumbly Top: 38
    Quick and Easy Flatbreads: 50
    Tin Can Bread: 49

R

Raisins
- Cinnamon Raisin Sourdough: 110
- Tin Can Bread: 49

Relish
- BBQ, Pickled Corn and Peppers, Sausage: 152
- Quick Pickled Corn & Chili Pepper Relish: 125, 152

S

Sandwiches
- Grilled Soft Pretzel with Turkey and Cheese: 129
- Open-Face Tomato Sandwich: 130
- Focaccia BLT: 133
- The Summer Classic Burger: 141

Scones
- Chocolate Cherry Almond Scones: 41

Salad stuff
- Croutons: 33, 120, 123, 127
- Fried Green Tomatoes with Pickled Corn & Peppers: 124
- Watermelon, Tomato Panzanella: 127
- Heirloom Tomato Vinaigrette: 127

Señorita Bread
- Señorita Bread: 46
- Señorita Bread Waffles: 159

Shaping: 13-14, 21, 37, 42, 57, 61, 71, 81-82, 88, 93-94, 106

Soft Pretzels & Pretzel Bites: 37

Sourdough
- Award-Winning Sourdough: 105-108
- Cheddar and Jalapeño Sourdough: 113
- Cinnamon Raisin Sourdough: 110
- Coconut, Cherry, and Walnut Sourdough: 112
- Lemon, Rosemary, and Pine Nut Sourdough: 111

Sourdough English Muffins: 114

Sourdough Starter: 9, 101, 103, 105, 114, 117

Spreads and Toppings
- Corn & Chile Peppers: 141
- Quick Pickled Corn & Chili Pepper Relish: 125, 152
- Japanese Eggplant Spread: 138
- Lemon Ricotta Spread: 137
- Sweet Pickle Rémoulade: 124

Starter: 9, 101, 103, 105, 114, 117

Strawberry Shortcake: 160

T

Tangzhong
- Hokkaido Milk Rolls: 45
- Japanese milk bread: 42, 45

Tin Can Bread: 49

Tiny Potato Party: 142

Toasts
- Avocado Toast: 132
- Corn, Chiles and Tomato Toasts: 134

Tomatoes
- Avocado Toast: 132
- Corn, Chiles and Tomato Toasts: 134
- Focaccia BLT: 133
- Fried Green Tomatoes with Pickled Corn & Peppers: 124
- Lemon, Rosemary, Tomato Focaccia: 81
- Open-Face Tomato Sandwich: 130
- The Summer Classic Burger: 141
- Watermelon, Tomato Panzanella: 127

V

Vinaigrette
- Heirloom Tomato Vinaigrette: 127

W

Waffles
- Señorita Bread Waffles: 159

White bread
- A Quick Breakdown of Baking a Loaf of Bread: 19-23
- Just a Loaf of White Bread: 26

Whipped cream
- Berry Bread Pudding: 146
- Señorita Bread Waffles: 159
- Strawberry Shortcake: 160

Wheat bread
- Whole Lotta Wheat Bread: 29

Whole wheat flour: 17, 29, 101, 105, 117

X

Xanthan gum: 17, 88, 93-94

Y

Yeast: 9, 13, 17-18, 20, 26, 29-30, 33, 37, 42, 45-46, 50, 54, 57, 61-62, 65-66, 69, 77-78, 81-82, 90, 93-94, 101, 164

www.ingramcontent.com/pod-product-compliance
Lightning Source LLC
Chambersburg PA
CBHW061258170426
43191CB00042B/2440